D1384787

The Siege of Detroit in 1763

MAJOR HENRY GLADWIN

From a portrait by an unknown artist.
Courtesy of the Detroit Public Library.

The Lakeside Classics

THE SIEGE OF DETROIT
IN 1763

The Journal of
Pontiac's Conspiracy
and
John Rutherfurd's Narrative
of a Captivity

EDITED BY

MILO MILTON QUAIFE

The Lakeside Press

R. R. DONNELLEY & SONS COMPANY

CHICAGO

Christmas, 1958

PUBLISHERS' PREFACE

WHILE the publishers of the Lakeside Classics have certain self-imposed restrictions in the selection of subject matter, they do enjoy wide latitude respecting time and location within their chosen field of Americana. So it is that they were able to make an excursion two years ago into the Southeast of the eighteenth century, to return last year to the familiar Southwest of the nineteenth, and change place and period this year to the Midwest of the eighteenth.

This year's Classic deals with an important event at a strategic location during an era most significant to the development of the Midwest. At this time, following the surrender of Canada in 1760, the English were taking the territory over from the French, which meant that traders and trappers would gradually be giving way to settlers and colonizers. That change was destined to have a heavy impact upon the Indians, as some of them no doubt dimly foresaw. Chief Pontiac's ability as a leader, extraordinary as it was, was not great enough to turn the irresistible forces of encroaching civilization. His attempt to do so gives us some of the most exciting and gruesome stories of the opening up of our country. That he should pick Detroit as his own scene of operations in his conspiracy to expel the British is not surprising. Detroit held, and continues to enjoy, a favored location on the water route to the West and central to what is now Ohio, Indiana and Michigan.

The Journal of Pontiac's Conspiracy itself is a vivid account of an exciting episode in the Indian Wars. Since it ends abruptly and without explanation before the end of the action, the publishers have taken the liberty to include a brief account of what happened thereafter for the benefit of readers not intimately acquainted with this period of history. The narrative of John Rutherfurd's captivity, itself a good story, adds interesting details to the picture of the siege, and since it has not been readily available, it has been included in this volume.

The Editor in his Historical Introduction deals fully with the background and authorship of both the Journal of Pontiac's Conspiracy and Rutherfurd's Narrative. The publishers are happy again to have Dr. Quaife's expert editorial talents at work on his forty-second Lakeside Classic. It seems particularly appropriate in that he has lived in Detroit many years and has a particular interest in and knowledge of its history. We add our thanks to the acknowledgments he makes, especially to the Burton Historical Collection of the Detroit Public Library.

The Company is happy to report completion of another successful year, especially in view of unsettled conditions in some areas of our economy. There was a shifting of our customers' requirements, some needing more of our services, others less, and some using them for the first time.

Plans for expansion are being vigorously pursued. The Company was particularly pleased to reach an agreement with the National Geographic Society to print their magazine, so widely respected for its editorial excellence and outstanding quality. Production will commence in 1959. A building in Chicago is being remodeled to provide space for this work, as another already has been for our Engineering and Purchasing functions. Additional warehouse space is under construction in both Chicago and Crawfordsville to permit more efficient handling of increased tonnage of product. At Willard, Ohio, an addition has been completed and equipment is being installed to enable that plant to produce book work in addition to telephone directories. At Warsaw, Indiana, construction of a plant and a training program have been started, to utilize more of the equipment acquired last year from the Crowell-Collier Publishing Company. This over-all program naturally increases considerably requirements for capital funds. To meet these a public sale of debentures was made successfully last spring.

We send this volume to our many friends among our patrons, suppliers, employees and others, believing this an appropriate form of greeting from a printer, engraver, and binder. In so doing we are most gratefully conscious that our growth and success over the years has been made possible in large part by these friends, and so resolve to explore and strive for new ways to serve and co-operate with them ever better. To you, a Merry Christmas and a Happy New Year!

The Publishers

Christmas, 1958

CONTENTS

ILLUSTRATIONS

HISTORICAL INTRODUCTION

THE Burton Historical Collection of the Detroit Public Library contains hundreds of thousands of manuscripts. If its custodians were to be asked which one of them they would endeavor to save in the event of an overwhelming disaster they would almost certainly name a faded and mutilated record which bears the simple title *Journal ou Dictation d'une Conspiration.* And if some wealthy private collector should seek to purchase it by offering the Library a check with the price left blank, to be filled in at its pleasure, the answer would undoubtedly be that no amount of money whatever would tempt the Library to part with it.

Yet the manuscript, which for convenience is called the Pontiac Journal (although it was not written by Pontiac nor is it his journal), was not always highly prized nor carefully guarded. On the contrary, until about the year 1832, almost seventy years after it had been written in 1763, its whereabouts and its custodian are unknown. Stories more or less legendary relate, however, that a French Canadian house in Detroit was being razed, when "hidden away between the walls or in some such romantic spot" the document was found. Apparently its value was recognized for some one took the trouble to preserve it. At one time Father Gabriel Richard, whose memory is still cherished in Detroit, was its guardian and he "probably" housed it in old St. Anne's Church. Following his death in 1832 Governor Lewis Cass acquired it.

Cass was an able administrator and an avid scholar, and one might reasonably assume that the safety of the manuscript was at last assured. That it was not, was no fault of his, for on February 28, 1838 he gave it to the ten-year-old Michigan Historical Society, of which he was a leading promoter. One of the Society's most active workers was Henry Rowe Schoolcraft, whom Cass had been instrumental in bringing from his New York home to Detroit a score of years earlier. Schoolcraft became an earnest student of Indian life and lore and over a period of forty years or more he authored or edited a prodigious quantity of material dealing with the exploration and geology of the western country, and with the red race in particular.

So it came about that Cass indirectly secured the preservation of the contents of the Pontiac Journal, if not the Manuscript itself, since Schoolcraft procured its translation into English by Professor Louis Fasquelle of the University of Michigan, and published it in 1854 as one of the documents in Part II of his massive compilation of *In-*

formation Respecting the History, Condition and Prospects of the Indian Tribes of the United States. . . .

With the passing away of the group of historically-minded enthusiasts who had founded the Michigan Historical Society in the 1830's that organization fell into decay. The approach of America's Centennial Year, however, created a renewed interest in the country's past, and in 1874 the Michigan State Pioneer Society, which still flourishes under a slightly augmented name, was organized. It soon began issuing a series of publications of pioneer and historical material which by 1929 numbered forty massive volumes. For the most part these were indifferently edited, yet they served the invaluable function of preserving and disseminating a vast quantity of historical material of widely varying scholarly interest and value. Eventually a "Committee of Historians" of the Society obtained the services of Rudolph Worch and Dr. Krusty, editors of the Jackson, Michigan, *Volksfreund*, to prepare a second translation of the Pontiac Journal, which was published in Volume VIII, pp. 266–329, of the Society's *Collections*, issued in 1886. In addition to the Journal, several old-age narratives concerning the siege of 1763, recorded by Charles C. Trowbridge in 1824, were published, all, it was explained, being "copies and translations of papers in the possession of the Society at Detroit."

In the self-same year, 1886, Mr. Charles I. Walker, a prominent lawyer and historical scholar of Detroit, who was acting as custodian of the books and manuscripts of the defunct Michigan Historical Society, presented them as a gift to the Detroit Public Library. Presumably the Pontiac Journal was one of the documents included in the gift, but since no list of the items transmitted to the Library was made, this can only be inferred.

If the Journal was not included in the papers given to the Library, one can only wonder why. Had Editors Worch and Krusty, its recent translators, neglected to return it to the Society's custodian; or had he for some reason unrecorded withheld it from the papers he gave to the Library? No one now living knows the answer to these questions, nor did any one seem to care, until eight years later when Charles Moore, then living in Washington and engaged in writing a life of Major Gladwin, in whose career he was deeply interested, wrote to a friend in Detroit requesting him to verify some minor detail by checking it with the Pontiac Journal. To the consternation of all who were concerned in the matter the Journal had disappeared.

A diligent search for it, conducted by Clarence M. Burton, who ranks as one of America's foremost historical collectors, and others, proved fruitless. All available clues and probable resting-places of the document were examined without result, and an editorial in the Detroit *Evening News* of July 23, 1894 bewailed the carelessness of certain historians who had permitted Michigan's most valuable historical document to disappear.

Another decade passed, when in 1905 Mr. Burton received a call from Edward K. Stimson, who was serving as agent for the property in Ecorse of Judge Halmer H. Emmons, one of Michigan's distinguished jurists, who had died in 1877. Stimson told Burton that the Judge's down-river home contained a great quantity of old letters and other papers, which had been looted by stamp collectors and which were likely soon to be destroyed. If Mr. Burton cared to have the papers he was welcome to them.

Mr. Burton did, and proceeding to Judge Emmons' home he gathered up seven barrels of papers, even using a pitchfork, according to one story, to facilitate the task of sorting them. Among the mass of papers on the floor lay an untidy-looking document which upon examination proved to be the long-lost Pontiac Journal. How it had come into the possession of the estate of Judge Emmons (who had died some eight years before Worch and Krusty made the second translation of it), or why, having done so, it was permitted to be thrown away as worthless, are questions that still remain unanswered.

To complete the story of the Manuscript's vicissitudes, Mr. Burton secured its third translation by Professor R. Clyde Ford of the Michigan State Normal College and himself paid for its publication in 1912, edited by his daughter, M. Agnes Burton. The manuscript itself, along with his entire historical collection, was given to the Detroit Public Library in 1914. After more than a century and a half the Journal had found a permanent home. In 1938 the Michigan Chapter, Daughters of Founders and Patriots of America, paid for its expert restoration and binding and in 1949 the same Society had a special leather case made for its further protection.[1]

But why, the reader may reasonably ask, is this mutilated record written by an anonymous author almost 200 years ago valued so highly? It is not enough to say in reply that it is a unique record of perhaps the most colorful episode in Detroit's two-and-a-half centuries of existence. Since three translations of the Journal have been published, preservation of its contents seems amply assured. This is true, also, of the contents of the Declaration of Independence, or of Lincoln's Gettysburg address and many another hallowed historical document. Quite apart from any prac-

[1] Data adapted from article by Helen H. Ellis, "A Mystery of Old Detroit" in Detroit Hist. Soc. *Bulletin,* IX, No. 1 (October, 1952).

tical consideration, such documents as these have a sentimental value which is priceless.

The Pontiac Journal is no literary masterpiece. On the contrary, its author violated almost every precept of literary composition. Despite this, however, he succeeded in creating an invaluable picture of an epochal conflict between the champions of primitive savagery and the upholders of civilized society. Pontiac, the red leader, was haughty, mercurial, cruel, and unscrupulous. His opponent, Major Gladwin, was his opposite in all these respects. His followers, too, were keyed to a state of conscious exaltation. Separated from their countrymen by hundreds of miles of wilderness, assailed by vastly superior numbers, with the prospect strong that they would be overwhelmed, and the certainty that in this event a hideous death awaited them, they resolved, in the words of one of their number, "to conduct ourselves like Englishmen."

What this meant finds concrete illustration in the down-river affair of September 3, when the schooner *Huron*, manned by Captain Horsey and an eleven-man crew, was assailed by night by 300 savages in a multitude of canoes. Swarming about the vessel, some got under the stern, thinking to climb through the cabin windows; others hung on the sides and bows, cutting and slashing with their tomahawks in the effort to make holes through which to rake the deck. Captain Horsey was slain and over half of his men were cut down, but the handful of survivors, casting aside their guns and seizing lances and spears, fought desperately on. After an hour of such fighting the savages abandoned the contest and melted away in the darkness. When two days later the *Huron* cast anchor before the Fort, the bayonets and spears on board were dyed with Indian blood "like axes in a slaughter house." "In short," wrote trader James Sterling four days later, "the attack was the bravest ever known to be made by Inds., and the Defense such as British subjects alone are capable of."[2]

The more immediate causes of the conflict at Detroit resulted from the circumstances attend-

[2]*Burton Hist. Coll. Leaflet,* VIII, 6–7 (September, 1929).

An old-age story of dubious validity, recorded long after the event, credited Adam Brown with participation in the attack upon the *Huron.* When the defenders seemed on the point of being overcome the mate called out to blow up the ship; Brown, who understood English, warned the Indians, who promptly fled overboard, thus ending the battle. Brown had been carried away in boyhood from his Virginia home. Brought to Detroit, he was adopted by a Huron squaw, who reared him as her son. He remained permanently among the Indians, and became a village chief. Brownstown Township in Wayne County preserves the name of his village, which for a

ing the closing years of the Seven Years' War.
Between 1689 and 1763 England waged four great
wars with France, to the accompaniment of extensive European alliances. Each of them, too,
had its American counterpart in which savages
from the Great Lakes and the Upper Mississippi
journeyed eastward to assist their French "Father" in ravaging the frontier English settlers. For
most practical purposes the last of the series—
the Seven Years' War—ended in North America
with the surrender of Canada to victorious General Amherst at Montreal on September 7, 1760.
But the formal conclusion of peace between the
two nations was delayed until the winter of 1763,
and the three-year delay proved fateful for the
happiness of Detroit. By the terms of the surrender of Canada the French settlers became subjects of Great Britain. Immediately following it,
General Amherst dispatched Major Robert Rogers with a small force to take over the French
posts around the Great Lakes. Detroit, the most
important one, was transferred to English rule on
November 29, 1760, and the remoter posts were
occupied the following year.

Meanwhile British traders swarmed over the

generation or more was a well-known stopping place for
travelers between Detroit and the Maumee. Descendants
of Brown still reside in Oklahoma and elsewhere. See
sketch in *The John Askin Papers*, I, 340.

country, eager to exploit the Indian trade. The French settlers bore no love for the newcomers, and the Indians, who had not been consulted in the surrender of their homeland, soon conceived a feeling of hatred for them. A plot for a general uprising against them was discovered and thwarted in 1761. But the conditions were ripe for its renewal, awaiting only the appearance of a suitable leader.

Upon such a stage strode the Ottawa chieftain, Pontiac, to animate his red followers with a ready-made program for the removal of their ills. In anticipation of the return of their vanquished French "Father" all of the English garrisons were to be overthrown and their followers either slaughtered or driven from the country. For himself, Pontiac reserved the destruction of Detroit, the most important of the western posts. Unfortunately for his design, however, one vital miscalculation was made. Quite reasonably, having in view his limited sources of information, he anticipated that the local French inhabitants would make common cause with him against the intruders. He could not know that even before his program was launched the definitive treaty of peace between France and England had been concluded at distant Paris. No longer could there be any hope that France would come to the support of Pontiac, and such individual Frenchmen as those who joined forces with him exposed themselves to the perils of treason.

The plight in which the French settlers found themselves during the siege deserves our sympathetic understanding. From the time of their remote ancestors they had been taught to look upon England as the national enemy. Now their country had been defeated in a great war, as one consequence of which they had been forcibly transformed into British subjects. That they entertained nostalgic longings for their restoration to France seems obvious. When Pontiac opened his attack upon the English, most of them sought to remain neutral spectators of the scene, although some responded to Pontiac's appeal to them to make common cause with him. Even today, the role of a neutral in time of war is a difficult one, as the United States regretfully learned in the years preceding the War of 1812. In Detroit in 1763 the majority of the bedeviled French settlers eventually organized for resistance to the increasing demands of Pontiac; one minor group joined the English, while another allied itself with Pontiac. In such a situation as they confronted, each individual must decide for himself where he will take his stand. In 1861 Robert E. Lee adhered to the Southern Confederacy. George H. Thomas, another eminent Virginian, remained loyal to the Union. Today, probably few persons would condemn either of them for the stand he elected to take. The French settlers of Detroit in 1763 were confronted with a like hard situation. Whatever stand they took as individuals their motives deserve our respectful consideration.

Let us return to the question of the identity of our unknown author. Obviously he was a Frenchman who was in Detroit throughout the siege. Presumably this implies that he was one of the local settlers. Mr. Burton, having eliminated the two local priests from consideration, fixes upon Robert Navarre, "the Scrivener," as the author of the Journal. Professor Ford, having dwelt upon the possibilities in the case, concludes with the frank admission that he is baffled by the problem of identification. So also is the present Editor, but certain pertinent considerations may be worth noting.

In any criminal investigation the determination of the motive of the culprit becomes the foremost consideration. From the first page of the Journal we discover that its author disliked and despised Pontiac. From succeeding pages we discover a similar dislike for the "bad" Huron band which supported Pontiac, and for the French "renegades" who rallied to his cause. Apparently he resided within the fort, where he enjoyed direct access to whatever transpired from day to day. Obviously, too, he was a warm adherent to the cause of the beleaguered garrison. All this, however, does not suffice us to fix upon his identity. If it be suggested that the writer sought to curry official English favor, we are compelled to ask what favor would Navarre, from the known circumstances of his career, have expected or desired? To which there is no obvious answer.

A further puzzle is encountered when we consider the literary character of the narrative. As Professor Ford makes clear, it is written very badly indeed. This fact excludes the two priests, both of them educated men, of course, from consideration as the possible authors. But Navarre was also an educated man (precisely how well educated we do not know) and the reasoning which removes the priests from consideration seems to apply with like force to Navarre, the Scrivener.

The founder of Detroit was a brilliant man of pronounced literary ability. But for this exception, literary talent or preoccupation in French Detroit was far from common. How are we to explain the zeal which impelled our author to devote laborious days, and probably weeks, to the task, subsequent to the siege, of expanding what must have been the relatively meager daily entries in his diary to the proportions they assume in the Journal before us? And if the writer in question was not Navarre, who else among the French settlers had reason for undertaking such a task?

Emile Gaboriau, father of the modern literary school of detective fiction, propounded several rules of procedure for solving criminal mysteries. Firstly, be suspicious of that which seems probable; examine carefully that which seems improbable, or even impossible. Neither Mr. Burton nor Professor Ford seems to have given sufficient attention to this rule. Instead, they assume that the author was a local resident, and endeavor to find among the residents of Detroit the one who wrote the Journal. But one of the first victims of Pontiac was an English nobleman, Sir Robert Davers, who for some reason known only to wandering Englishmen was paying a visit to this obscure corner of the globe. Davers was killed and so his name became embalmed in the local history of the siege. May it not be possible that another traveler, of French origin, whose presence has escaped contemporary record, was also visiting Detroit in 1763, and that he found reason to record its story? Or may not one of the many traders who journeyed between Detroit and Montreal or Quebec have done so? If so, there is no difficulty in suggesting the motive which probably animated his pen; namely, the desire to curry favor with some official of the conquering race—perhaps some British army officer, whose authority could be directed to promote or to destroy his commercial enterprise.[3]

The first and second editions of the Journal were published in English translation only, with but meager editorial care. The third edition, brought out by Mr. Burton in 1912, still remains the only scholarly printing of the Journal. He had it freshly translated by an able scholar, Professor R. Clyde Ford of the Ypsilanti State Normal College, and both the translation and the French original were printed on facing pages. In addition, for the first time the Journal was carefully edited by Mr. Burton's daughter Agnes, who was thoroughly steeped in Detroit's history.

Unfortunately, however, only a small number of copies was printed and no index to the contents was provided. Special scholars who are not

[3]This suggestion seems more probable than that a visiting French traveler authored the Journal. Presumably such a person would have possessed an adequate literary command of his native language. An English trader, however, whose formal education was slight and whose limited knowledge of French had been acquired in the course of his trading contacts, might be expected to be sadly deficient in his mastery of the literary language. Many of the British traders at Detroit possessed more or less knowledge of French. For one such person see *post,* 123.

content with the Ford translation will still have need to resort to the Burton edition of the Journal. For the great majority of readers, however, Professor Ford's scholarly translation will prove sufficient. The centuries-long story of white-Indian conflict still remains as thrilling as anything in American history, and the present publication of the Pontiac Journal will for the first time make one of its most notable episodes accessible to thousands of readers.

Prominent among the traders who swarmed over Canada following the conquest was a group of men, several of whom had been army officers, who associated themselves in a partnership and obtained from General Amherst the grant of 10,000 acres of land at the upper end of the Niagara Portage route between Lake Ontario and Lake Erie. One of the partners was Captain Walter Rutherfurd of the 62nd Regiment, who had located in New York. Another was James Sterling, a native of Ireland, who had served under General Haldimand during the war as Commissioner of Provisions.[4] Early in 1761 he erected a storehouse at Niagara, and in July moved on to Detroit in the capacity of western

---

[4]The remaining partners were James Syme of Schenectady; Lieutenant George Coventry of the 55th Regiment,

Superintendent of the Company's activities. Here he opened a store, dispatched trading ventures to Mackinac, the Maumee, and other tributary points, and endeavored to win the good will of the French settlers. In particular he paid successful suit for the hand of Angelique Cuillerier *dit* Beaubien, whose father was a prominent resident of Detroit and the half-brother of the Sieur de Bellestre, the late French commandant.

Captain Walter Rutherfurd had a nephew, John Rutherfurd, who was born in Yorkshire in 1746. Orphaned in infancy, he was reared by his grandfather, Sir John Rutherfurd of Roxburghshire, Scotland. At the age of sixteen he was consigned to the care of his Uncle in New York, who presently dispatched him to Sterling at Detroit. Thus it came to pass that as a youth of seventeen he was precipitated into the savage turmoil of the Pontiac War. He had an excellent family background and had evidently acquired a fair education. Evidently, too, he possessed a high degree of intelligence and discretion. Hardy as a nine-lived cat, he survived his terrible experience and lived to a green old age. Fortunately, too, at the urging of a cousin, Sir John Nesbit,

also of Schenectady and Major John Duncan of the 44th Regiment. The latter was in Detroit during the siege and to him we are indebted for a valuable account of the battle of Bloody Run.

he wrote the vivid narrative of his experiences during the siege to whose contents the concluding portion of the present volume is devoted.

Unfortunately the original manuscript of Rutherfurd's narrative has long since disappeared. However, several long-hand copies of it were made at different times, and three of these are still known to exist. Two of them, owned by a great-grandson, Colonel Richard M. Raynsford of Milton Manor, Northampton, England, have been temporarily loaned to the present Editor; one, written in ink long faded, is contained in a large-sized record book which bears the notation of "Henry Rutherfurd, Bedford, 25th June, 1849."[5] Appended to the narrative itself is a short biographical note, attributed to Thomas Rutherfurd, son of the Author, who died at Fairnington on March 27, 1863. This is

[5]Concerning this, Colonel Raynsford writes: "How it came into my possession is a puzzle. My second sister was at Fairnington when my Uncle, Henry Rutherfurd, died. She did a lot in helping to settle up his estate. She presumably brought the notebook back to my mother's house in Gerrard's Cross. She died and my eldest sister came to live with me at Milton Manor and presumably brought the notebook with her. She died some years ago." Letter of June 17, 1957.

In a subsequent letter (Aug. 17, 1957) replying to a request for a specimen of Henry Rutherfurd's handwriting (for comparison with the manuscript) Colonel Raynsford states that application to Henry's two still-living daughters elicited the information that they have none;

followed by a medley of material concerning Rutherfurd and the war, headed "Appendix and Notes." Since several of the items are taken from Francis Parkman's book, first published in 1851, it seems evident that the copy was made subsequent to this time.

The second copy of the narrative owned by Colonel Raynsford is contained in a hard-cover record book whose contents are limited to the narrative and Thomas Rutherfurd's brief biographical note. The ink is not faded, and the contents of the document are substantially identical with those of the larger notebook copy.

Henry Rutherfurd was a son of Thomas, and a grandson of the Author. In 1878 Bookseller H. S. Martin of Berwick-on-Tweed published Rutherfurd's narrative and the additional biographical sketch as a 45-page pamphlet to which was added the note, "Copied at Bangalore, July 13, 1867." Fourteen years later, in 1892, the President of the Royal Canadian Institute reported to its members the acquisition of an un-

that Henry Rutherfurd died at the age of 96 and during his latter years did very little writing. One of the daughters, however, added that she thinks her father asked his sister, Miss Ellen Rutherfurd, to copy the manuscript for him. If this recollection is valid, it implies that the original manuscript was then in grandson Henry Rutherfurd's possession. "But where [it] now is," concludes Colonel Raynsford, "the devil only knows, and I fear we shall never get hold of it."

published manuscript of the Pontiac War written by Lieutenant Rutherfurd of the Black Watch Regiment. He further explained that the copy (subsequently published in the Society's *Transactions*, Vol. III, 229-52) had been made by Colonel Thomas Rutherfurd of the Madras Staff Corps, recently Commandant of Delhi, who had given it to Thomas Hodgkins, by whom it had now been presented to the Institute. Evidently the President had never heard of the Berwick-on-Tweed pamphlet publication of 1878, yet comparison of the two printings discloses that they are almost identical copies of each other. Significantly, the Institute copy omits the note (appended to the other) "Copied at Bangalore, July 13, 1867." Colonel Thomas W. Rutherfurd was a brother of Henry, both being sons of Thomas, who died in 1863. The Royal Canadian Institute has long since ceased to exist and a search instituted by the present Editor some thirty years ago for its copy of Rutherfurd's narrative proved futile. The close identity between the contents of Henry Rutherfurd's large notebook copy, the smaller one owned by Colonel Raynsford, and the two printed versions of 1878 and 1893 suggest a common relationship which I am at a loss to unravel.

In so far as most of our readers are concerned this will not matter. Our present copy of the

narrative, recently procured in England by Miss
Emily Driscoll of New York City, was made at
Wells by M. Rutherfurd in October, 1787. The
decision to include the narrative in the 1958
Lakeside Classics volume had already been
reached, and the task of editing the Royal
Canadian Institute version had been completed
when opportunely in the spring of 1957 Miss
Driscoll's discovery was reported. The desira-
bility of substituting it for the version hitherto
printed was evident, and having learned that
Miss Driscoll had granted the *American Heritage*
permission to publish it, arrangements were made
with its Editor to have the present writer edit
the document for that publication, in return for
which permission to reproduce it in the Lakeside
Classics volume was granted.

The narrative was published in the April, 1958
issue of the magazine, and its present reprinting
constitutes the fourth publication of Rutherfurd's narrative. Copies of the 1878 and 1893
printings are so obscure, however, that the
American Heritage printing is the first to command any considerable number of readers.[6] In
preparing it for publication I have deemed it
undesirable to reproduce the many peculiarities

[6]The only existing copy of the 1878 pamphlet known
to the present Editor was procured by the Library of
Congress from Colonel Raynsford as recently as 1953.

of punctuation, vocabulary, spelling, and composition of the manuscript copy. Consequently, I have exercised as complete freedom to transform it into readable literary form as a careful regard for preserving the meaning of the original copy has permitted. This treatment implies no reflection, however, upon the ability of the youthful Author, who has himself explained the difficulty under which he wrote. Aside from this consideration, the literary style deemed acceptable two centuries ago demands frequent modification to make it acceptable to the present-day reader.

I am indebted to many persons whose assistance has made possible the editing of the present volume: first of all, to the late Clarence M. Burton and the late Professor Ford for their joint creation of the indispensable 1912 edition of the, Pontiac Journal; secondly, to Mrs. Elleine Stones until recently chief of the Burton Historical Collection of the Detroit Public Library, and to her staff of co-workers for assistance and courtesies too numerous to detail; in this connection the contribution of Miss Helen H. Ellis in recording the history of the Pontiac Manuscript should be particularly noted; thirdly, to Lieutenant-

Files of the *Transactions* of the Royal Canadian Institute are available to scholars in certain reference libraries, but their existence is unknown to the general public.

Colonel Richard M. Raynsford, great-grandson of Rutherfurd, for his generous response to my many questions concerning his ancestor, and in particular for supplying a photograph of Lieutenant Rutherfurd's portrait and the two manuscript copies of his narrative which have been noted above; fourthly, to the President of The Lakeside Press, Mr. Gaylord Donnelley, and his co-workers for their cooperation in promoting my editorial work; fifthly, to my wife, Letitia, for her customary patient secretarial assistance in transforming my copy into readable form; and finally, to Dr. Howard H. Peckham, Director of the William L. Clements Library of the University of Michigan, for the guidance afforded by his excellent book, *Pontiac and the Indian Uprising*, published in 1947.

M. M. QUAIFE

Detroit, April, 1958

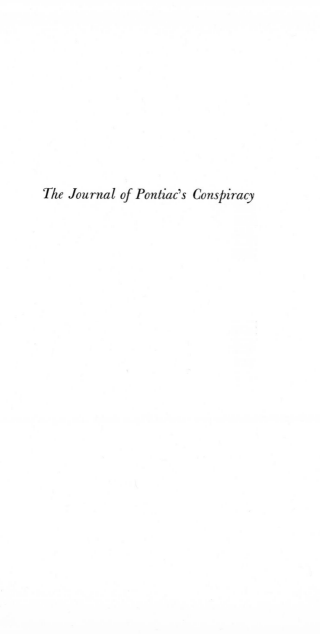

The Journal of Pontiac's Conspiracy

Journal of
Pontiac's Conspiracy
1763

Published by
CLARENCE MONROE BURTON
Under the Auspices of the
Michigan Society of the Colonial Wars
Edited by M. Agnes Burton

PREFACE

THE Pontiac Manuscript, or Journal, has for years been considered the most important document in existence containing an account of the conspiracy of the Ottawa chief. It has twice been translated and is the foundation of various novels and dramas picturing the times of the French and Indian War. It is the document upon which Francis Parkman so cleverly built his history of the events of 1763. Its history so far as known has been related by Parkman and by others, and many conjectures have been made regarding its authorship. That it was originally the work of a Frenchman is evident throughout. The apparent anxiety to place the French in a favorable light, to explain their difficult position and justify their actions, could only have been expressed by a Frenchman. His knowledge of the happenings within and without the fort, his familiarity with the motives and actions of Pontiac, is sufficient proof that he was a Frenchman of influence both with the Indians and the English. His description of the minute details attending Pontiac's councils makes it impossible to doubt the author's presence on those occasions.

The manuscript was thought to have been written by the assistant priest of St. Anne's

Church, and the fact that the manuscript was at one time owned by Father Gabriel Richard, the priest who was in charge of the same church from 1798-1832, adds color to this conjecture. A comparison, however, with the writing of that priest still preserved in St. Anne's records destroys that theory. Prof. Ford thinks that it was written by some one within the fort, and suggests Robert Navarre. Following this suggestion, a comparison of this document with many of the extant records in the hand of Navarre seems to point to a satisfactory solution. Specimens of the journal, a page from St. Anne's Records and a deed by Navarre are given herewith for the purposes of comparison. A close examination of each shows similarity between the journal and the Navarre deed. The writer is not as neat and painstaking in his journal as in his public papers, but the same style and form of writing is found in every line. He has evidently kept an accurate chronology of daily events, but has from day to day turned back and filled in with more minute details, as for example the description of the conduct of Luneau on pp. 118-20, and many similar passages.

Although Navarre did not reside within the fort, his easy access in the performance of his duties gave him the complete knowledge of affairs within.

He was a man of some education, had been the Royal Notary of the place under French rule and hoped to continue in a similar office after the British came. He was recommended by the British Commandant as worthy of confidence and was retained to conduct many of the duties of the post where both the English and the French were concerned. His long career in active service, begun in 1734, had made him thoroughly familiar with the languages of the Indians, for whom he frequently acted as interpreter. At the time of the siege he was living on his farm on the southwest side of the village. This farm is now within the limits of the city of Detroit and bears the name of Navarre or Brevoort farm, about two miles below the center of the city.[1] The land was formerly occupied by the Potawatomi Indians and was given by that tribe to their friend, Robert Navarre, whom they affectionately called

---

[1] The Brevoort farm, legally described as Private Claim No. 20, lies immediately west of the entrance to the Ambassador Bridge, between Twenty-First and Twenty-Fourth streets. Here was the site of the Potawatomi village, and in the French period the vicinity was known as the Coast of the Potawatomies. In 1772 the tribe ceded the cemetery site to Robert Navarre the Younger forever, "that he may cultivate the same, light a fire thereon and take care of our dead." In this instance "forever" proved to mean something less than a century. The extension of Woodbridge Street in the late sixties involved the desecration of the cemetery.

"Robiche." Jean Marie Alexis Navarre, a son of Robert Navarre, was born and baptized at the house of his parents, and not in the church, on Sept. 22, 1763. The child was born on the night of his baptism, and the church entry was made the following day. This appears from the record and indicates the freedom the members of the Navarre family had in entering the besieged town. Therefore it seems quite plausible to attribute the journal to Robert Navarre.

Before leaving the subject the Editor wishes to add a word concerning Sir Robert Davers. In the *Acts of the Privy Council, Colonial Series, Vol. 1745–1766*, under the date of Aug. 31, 1763, there is a petition of Sir Robert Davers to the Board of Trade for a grant of Grosse Isle and several other little islands surrounding it, Isle Aux Dinde and lands on the eastern shore of the Detroit River from Lake Erie on the south to the River Aux Canards on the north. Sir Robert was killed before the petition was referred to the Board, as recorded in the diary, and the Indians made use of some of these islands during the siege.

C. M. BURTON

Detroit, Nov., 1912.

TRANSLATOR'S PREFACE

THE so-called Pontiac Manuscript is an intensely illuminating document for its gossip, information, and folk lore, and the various sidelights which it throws on the memorable siege of Detroit by the Indians in 1763, but it is historical rather than literary, as even the most hasty reader will perceive. As translator I have been concerned to reproduce the original in an intelligible, if not elegant English, and at the same time to leave untouched as much as possible the verbosity, discursiveness, and repetitions which are so characteristic of the early work. However, what Pope called the "illiteracies" will not appear, though interwoven all through with the rhetorical peculiarities: the unknown writer displays such an utter indifference to matters of punctuation, spelling, composition, and grammar that it would be hazardous to attempt to perpetuate any of his vagaries. Still, it is certain that they have added greatly to the task of translation. Through the fact that capital letters are used so indiscriminately, and punctuation is so neglected and capricious, it is frequently difficult to tell where phrases or sentences end or begin; and then, outside of the traditional combinations the spelling is surprisingly phonetic, which helps to make the reading of many passages and parts quite a *tour de force*.

The question of the authorship of the manuscript has been a subject of speculation at different times, but nothing definite has ever been established. Parkman in his *Conspiracy of Pontiac* draws upon the facts of the manuscript which he knew through a copy loaned him by Gen. Lewis Cass, and he makes the statement that it is "conjectured to be the work of a French priest." Since he makes general acknowledgment of his indebtedness to Gen. Cass for materials dealing with the war and Detroit, one may infer, I think, that he was merely endorsing a tradition which was current in the French family who were in possession of the document in Gen. Cass' time.

It is well known that there were only two priests at Detroit during the period of the siege: Father Pierre Potier, Jesuit missionary to the Hurons, whose mission was on what is now the Canadian side of the river; and Father Simple Bocquet, a Franciscan, who was in charge of St. Anne's Church, within the enclosure of the Fort.[2]

[2]Pierre Potier was born at Blandain, Flanders, April 21, 1708. He entered the Jesuit Order and in 1743 was sent to Canada, where he devoted a year at Lorette to the study of the Huron language. In 1744 he came to Detroit as assistant to Father La Richardie, who had served the Hurons here since 1728. At this time the Huron village was immediately west of the fort, near the foot of present-

Now as to Father Potier: There are several specimens of his composition and writing extant

day Third Street, on a site now included in the Civic Center. Owing to tribal discord, about the year 1738 Father La Richardie led the band to Bois Blanc (Bob Lo) Island near the mouth of the Detroit River. It was here, therefore, that Father Potier began his mission work among them. In 1747, during the absence of La Richardie at Quebec, a faction led by Chief Nicolas destroyed the mission buildings and plotted the entire destruction of the garrison and settlement of Detroit. Fortunately a Christian squaw disclosed the plot and, as in 1763, De Longueuil, the Commandant, took effective measures to prevent its execution. He now required the Hurons to settle closer to the Fort, where he might more effectively control them. Accordingly they were relocated at Montreal Point on the South, or Canadian side of the River. The site is immediately below the Canadian exit from the Ambassador Bridge. Here in the town of Sandwich, oldest on the Canadian side of the River, the Church of the Assumption and Assumption College (now a University) subsequently developed. Huron Line Road, which passes alongside the Church, marks the former eastern boundary of the Huron village. Here Father Potier, the last Jesuit serving the western missions, was found dead before his fireplace, July 16, 1781. Data adapted from Thwaites, (Ed.) *The Jesuit Relations*, LXIX, 289; George Paré, *The Catholic Church in Detroit* 1701–1888 (Detroit, 1951) 182–90.

Although Father Simple Bocquet came to Canada in 1743, information concerning his activities is lacking until his arrival at Detroit on August 10, 1754 to serve either as assistant to Father Bonaventure in charge of the parish of St. Anne, or as his successor in charge of it. At any rate his Detroit ministry began on this date. It ended with his retirement to Quebec, borne down by the infirmities of old age, in 1782. There he died on March 24, 1787. See George Paré', *The Catholic Church in Detroit*, index entries

and nowhere do they show the least resemblance
to the hand of the Pontiac Manuscript. Father
Potier wrote an almost uncial script, and a page
of his writing reminds one of the painstaking
efforts of some mediaeval copyist. The Pontiac
Manuscript, on the other hand, is in the ordinary
running hand which was the pride of the French
writers of the eighteenth century.

Father Potier was something of a scholar, also;
he composed a grammar of the Huron language
which is full of Latin terminology, and the regis-
try of baptisms in his parish he kept in Latin,—
all of which goes to show, it seems to me, that
he would hardly be guilty of such egregious language errors as the Pontiac Manuscript abounds
in. It is hard to imagine a man with any sort of
Latin training using in his mother tongue singular verbs for plurals and vice versa, or disre-
garding the commonest gender agreements, or
composing sentences so loose and rambling in
structure as frequently to be almost inane. The
fact is, the good father did not write French that
way. For many years he kept a *Livre de Compte*,
or account book, of the business transactions of
his mission, and while he treated the matter of
capital letters with some startling liberality, his
spelling and syntax are quite reliable. Another
point: Whenever he signs his name in the records it is always *Potier*, yet the writer of the

manuscript frequently, commonly, in fact, refers to him as *Poitier*. Now I do not believe he would all at once have developed such carelessness in regard to his own name, even in his old age.

Another point: According to Elliott's[3] investigations into the history of the Jesuit missions at Detroit, Father Potier enjoyed the very closest friendship with Jean Baptiste Meloche who lived up above the Fort and was Pontiac's intimate and adviser, and he was himself on friendly terms with him. Now, though it is certain that among all the *habitants* of the region Meloche was deepest in Pontiac's councils, it is equally plain that the writer of the Manuscript had no regard for Pontiac, as is evident from more than one statement which characterizes him as murderous, treacherous, dishonest, and pagan.

The greatest argument, however, against Father Potier's authorship of the Manuscript is the internal evidence of the document itself which, in my opinion, points unmistakably to some writer within the Fort who, through the intercourse which was constantly kept up between the French of the village and stockade and the settlers up and down the river, and the friendly relations which were enjoyed with the Indians, knew all that was going on and was thus

[3]Richard R. Elliott, local historian and citizen.

able to discuss and describe events with a surprising show of familiarity.

Still, when one comes to examine the Manuscript carefully it is seen that there is a marked
difference in the treatment of various parts; oc-
currences and doings among the Indians are
sketched with seeming fidelity and objectivity,
yet with a knowledge which might easily have
been gained from rumor and gossip circulating
among the French and Indians; on the other
hand, everything which has to do with the life
of the garrison, especially in the martial aspect
of events as they unroll from day to day, is given
with all possible detail and circumstance. In fact,
the atmosphere is the atmosphere of the Fort,
and the viewpoint that of an eyewitness. Chit-
chat about this and that; such statements as "It
was brought to the knowledge of the Commandant at three o'clock," or "At five o'clock it was
known in the Fort by a Frenchman who had gone
out," or "News reached the Fort at four o'clock";
the exact number of men who engaged in the
various sorties; all the interesting and loquacious
details of the erection of the *cavalier* or portable
bastion; such turns as "The Indians *came* to fire
on the Fort," etc.; the thickness of planking in
certain boats and the length of chains used with
grappling hooks; casual reference to the fact that
people heard shots fired in this or that direction,

—all this and much more like it helps to weave a tissue of petty detail which is so significant as a whole. It is therefore pretty certain that the Fort is the real locus of the composition.

Now, who of all the French within the Fort might have been the author of the manuscript? When this question is asked everyone thinks at once of Father Bocquet, the Recollect curate of St. Anne's, for he was in the very center of events and abundantly qualified to write a most interesting story. But did he do so?

With Father Bocquet, as with Father Potier, it is a question of scholarship which is the disturbing one. As one reads over the records of St. Anne's Church left by Father Bocquet one is struck by their clearness and exactness; they are carefully made. And on those occasions where there was reason for more than the stereotyped statements he writes with a command of the language and an observance of its forms which are entirely lacking in the manuscript. In fact, it would seem quite impossible that the hand which wrote the accurate parish register could be the same one which composed the rambling and more or less illiterate story of the siege.[4]

[4]The St. Anne Parish Register has been kept since the founding of the city in 1701. Save for the one at St. Augustine, Florida it is the oldest continuous Catholic

The author of the journal-like narrative makes mention of the church holy days as they come along, but with one singular omission: he notes Sunday, May 22, as Pentecost, but no attention is called to the fact that the following Sunday, May 29, is Trinity Sunday (fête de la Trinité), though he records again that Thursday, June 2, is Corpus Christi Day, and June 9 is Little Corpus Christi Day. The church records give ample evidence that Father Bocquet was exact and painstaking in his churchly duties, and even the Pontiac Manuscript bears witness in more than one place to his punctilious regard for church observances; it seems, therefore, hard to believe that he would have neglected an important entry like that in his journal, surrounded as it was with other festival days. Undoubtedly the narrative was composed after the siege, either from memoranda or brief diarial notes, but this would make such an oversight in a well-trained priest just as unlikely.

Again the question recurs, Who *did* write the Pontiac Manuscript? And after having spun my theories so far I am compelled to acknowledge

parish register in the United States. A translation of its contents down to about the year 1830, made in recent years by George Paré, scholarly historian of the Diocese of Detroit, may be found in the Burton Historical Collection of the Detroit Public Library.

that no one knows. One of Goethe's characters in his *Iphigenia* says:

"Much talking is not needed to refuse,
The other hears in all naught but the No!"

And probably some who have followed this fore-word so far will think the same. The elimination of the two priests from likelihood of the author-ship has not solved the problem, however much it may have narrowed it down. It draws the cor-don, as it were, a little tighter around the Fort, but as in the days of the siege there is still plenty of opportunity for the Frenchman to escape. And so far he has done so.

In all probability, if the manuscript were intact to-day, or if what is left were perfectly whole and legible, the identity of the writer would be dis-closed; it is quite likely that many marginal notes are missing, as some even now are almost if not quite obscured. And it is quite likely, too, that the missing pages of the conclusion of the manu-script may have held the writer's name, for it does not sound like an anonymous document.

Now if I were to hazard a conjecture as to the author I should say it was probably—notice the probably—Robert Navarre, "The Scrivener," once sub-intendant and notary at Fort Pontchar-train for the French king, and in the days of the British occupation still keeping the notarial rec-

ords. The manuscript is entirely silent about
him, a very significant fact, it seems to me, for he
was exceedingly well known and prominent in
the affairs of the settlement. He was a man of
parts, with an intelligence half literary, half military, and especially well fitted to appreciate all
that was happening around him.

I cannot close this little disquisition without
expressing a translator's joy over the many quaint
and curious words and phrases which I have
come upon in the perusal of the old document.
The French of Detroit in that early day, shut
away as the post was from intercourse with the
mother country, was in many respects the French
of an older period, with a large number of special
words and phrases which had come from life in
the wilderness. Twice in the manuscript occurred
the word *sacquaquois*, used with a feeling quite
French; but though the word was evidently Galli-
cized it was just as plainly not French. Suspecting that it was Indian I submitted it to a Chippewa friend who on more than one occasion has
helped me in similar difficulties; he recognized
the word at once from its Chippewa cognate as
meaning a "yell or shout of victory."

This old story of the siege of Detroit is a
chronicle out of an age long past, and yet it is a
story with so much human interest in it that it
ought to prove fascinating reading to the descend-

ants of those first settlers of Detroit, and to all others who call themselves the city's children. Mr. Burton, by bringing it to public notice again and putting it within the reach of every one, is doing a real service to the people of Detroit and the commonwealth.

R. Clyde Ford

Ypsilanti, Mich.
Dec. 25, 1910.

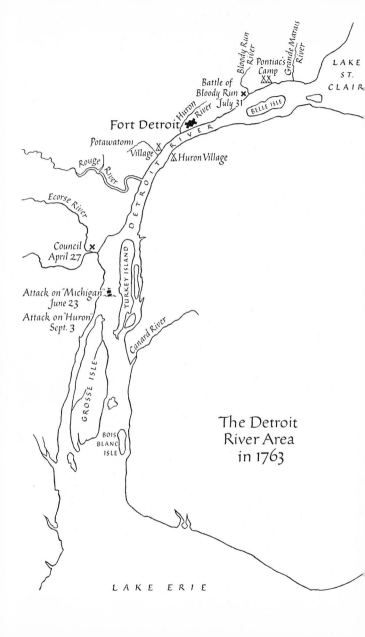

The Journal of
Pontiac's Conspiracy

OF THE INDIANS AGAINST THE ENGLISH, AND OF
THE SIEGE OF FORT DETROIT BY FOUR
DIFFERENT NATIONS
BEGINNING MAY 7, 1763

PONTIAC,[5] great chief of all the Ottawas,
Chippewas, Potawatomies, and all the nations of the lakes and rivers of the North, was a
proud, vindictive, war-like, and easily offended
man. Under pretext of some fancied insult from

[5]Much has been written about Pontiac although his
personal history, for obvious reasons, is obscure. Chiefly
he claims historical remembrance because of the role he
played in the uprising of the Indians of the Great Lakes
area against the British in 1763. Until recent years practically all that was written about him derived from Francis
Parkman's brilliant narrative, the *History of the Conspiracy
of Pontiac*, first published in 1851. His account of the
siege of Detroit in 1763 was chiefly based upon the
manuscript journal herein reproduced, supplemented by
local information derived from Lewis Cass and other old-
time Detroit residents. More recent scholarly investigations have served to modify in various respects the conception of Pontiac's role in the uprising entertained by
Parkman. For a brief sketch of Pontiac's career see
the *Dictionary of American Biography*. For a fuller, and
possibly definitive, study see Howard H. Peckham,
Pontiac and the Indian Uprising (Princeton University,
1947).

Mr. Gladwin,[6] Commandant of the Fort, he concluded that, inasmuch as he was the great chief of all the nations of the North, only himself and members of his own nation ought to occupy this part of the world, where for some sixty-odd

[6]Major Henry Gladwin was born in Derbyshire, Nov. 19, 1729. In 1753 he joined the 48th Foot Regiment and served throughout the entire American phase of the Seven Years' War. He was wounded while serving under General Braddock in 1755 and he attended General Amherst's campaign against Montreal in 1760. In June, 1761 Amherst dispatched him with a force of troops to visit and garrison the newly-acquired western posts which the French had surrendered. He arrived at Detroit in September suffering from malaria, and within a few weeks returned to command Fort William Augustus on the St. Lawrence near present-day Ogdensburg, New York. In August, 1762 he resumed command at Detroit, where he remained until the summer of 1764, meanwhile repulsing every effort of Pontiac to destroy the post. In him the forest chieftain had encountered a superb example of England's bull-dog breed of soldiers who for generations have maintained her rule in the far corners of the world. Wearied at last by almost a decade of wilderness service he asked to be relieved of his post. Returning to his Derbyshire home he followed the life of a country gentleman until his death on June 22, 1791. He had declined to serve in the American Revolution, although until 1780 his name was carried on the army list as "Deputy Adjutant General in America." Data adapted from Howard H. Peckham, *Pontiac and the Indian Uprising*. A direct descendant of Major Gladwin, Sir (Hubert Miles) Gladwyn Jebb, born in 1900, has devoted his career to the diplomatic service. From 1950 to 1954 he represented Great Britain at the United Nations in New York, subsequently serving as British ambassador to France.

years the French had lived for purposes of trade, and which the English had governed for three years by virtue of the conquest of Canada. This chief, and his whole nation for that matter, whose only bravery lies in the treachery which he is able to inspire by his suave exterior, resolved within himself to wrest the lands away from the English and the French people.

In order to succeed in his project which he had not as yet communicated to any of his nation, the Ottawas, Pontiac enlisted them in his cause by an address, and they did not hesitate to obey him, all inclined to wickedness as they are.[7] But as they alone were too weak for this enterprise the Chief tried by means of a council to draw over to his side the Potawatomies. This nation was controlled by a chief named Ninivois, a weak and easily influenced man; and knowing that Pontiac was his superior chief and treacherous, he and his whole tribe joined him. The two

[7]Over a century earlier the French explorer, Pierre Radisson, characterized the Ottawas as "the coursedest, unablest, the [most] infamous and cowar(d)liest" people he had seen among the four-score nations he had visited. *Voyages* (Boston, 1885), 203. Charles Stuart, an English captive at Detroit from 1755 to 1757, who had excellent reasons for his judgment, characterized them as "a Barbarous, Savage Nation and very wicked," continuing with a recital of shocking atrocities perpetrated by them following the defeat of General Braddock's army in 1755. See *Miss. Valley Hist. Rev.*, XIII 74–75.

nations together comprised about four hundred men. This number not yet seeming large enough, it was a question of drawing into their project the Hurons who were divided into two bands under two different chiefs of different character. However, the same Jesuit father, their missionary, controlled them both.

The two chiefs of this latter nation were called the one Takay, who was like Pontiac in character, the other Teata, who was a very cautious and extremely prudent man. The last named, not of a disposition to do wrong, was not easily won over. Not caring to listen to Pontiac's messengers he sent them back as they had come. They then went to the other band of the Hurons who listened to them and received from them war-belts to join Pontiac and Ninivois, the Ottawa and Chippewa chiefs; and it was voted by means of wampum which even distant savages use for adornment that there would be a council on the 27th of April, when the day and hour of the attack would be fixed, and the necessary measures determined in order that their plans might not be discovered. And so it was decided in the way I have mentioned before that the council should be held on the 15th of the moon,—a way of reckoning time among the Indians—which was Wednesday, the 27th of April.

When the day agreed upon for the council had

arrived, the Potawatomies, led by Ninivois, and the Hurons by Takay, betook themselves to the rendezvous which was on the Ecorse River ten miles from the fort toward the southwest,—a place which Pontiac had chosen for his camp at the breaking up of the winter so as not to be disturbed in his schemes. This move which was something new for him and his people caused the French to wonder, without, however, enabling them to see the reason for it, because the Indians are very whimsical anyway.

The council of the three nations, Ottawas, Potawatomies, and the bad Huron band, took place and was presided over by Pontiac in his capacity of head chief of all the northern nations. He made a speech, and as a reason for his action exhibited war-belts which he claimed he had received from his Great Father, the King of France, to induce him to attack the English. He also spoke of pretended insults which he and his nation had received from the Commandant and the English officers, and even mentioned how a sentinel had struck one of his followers with a gun while pursuing a woman who was his cousin.

They listened to him as chief, and in order to flatter his vanity and excite his pride they promised to do whatever he wished. Delighted to find so much loyalty among the three nations, which numbered four hundred and sixty men, he craftily made use of their weakness to get complete control over them. To accomplish this he related in the council the story of a Wolf Indian, who had journeyed to Heaven and talked with the Master of Life.[8] He spoke with so much eloquence that his narrative had just the effect upon them that he desired.

This story deserves a place here since it contains in blackest aspect the reason of the attack upon the English, and upon the French too, perhaps, if God in His mercy had not disposed differently. It is as follows:

An Indian of the Wolf nation, eager to make the acquaintance of the Master of Life,—this is the name for God among all the Indians—re-

[8]"Loups" or "Wolves" was the name applied by the French to the Confederacy known to the English as the Delawares, formerly the most important Algonquian group. In 1682 their council fire was maintained at Philadelphia, where William Penn concluded with them his well-known treaty. Overcome by the Iroquois and crowded by the whites, in the first half of the eighteenth century they migrated westward to the upper Ohio Valley. From about 1750 until the Treaty of Greenville in 1795 they were the most active opponents of the advancing tide of white settlement in the upper Ohio area.

Throughout the era of white-Indian conflict numerous "prophets" have served the role of voicing the Indian aspirations. One such prophet was the southern Ohio Delaware Indian whose vision Pontiac now adapted to serve the end of inciting his followers. For a more adequate account of the Delaware prophet's teaching see Peckham, *Pontiac and the Indian Uprising*, Chaps. 7 and 8.

solved to undertake the journey to Paradise, where he knew He resided, without the knowledge of any of his tribe or village. But the question was how to succeed in his purpose and find the way thither. Not knowing anyone who had been there and was thus able to teach him the road, he had recourse to incantation in the hope of deriving some good augury from his trance. As a rule all the Indians, even those who are enlightened, are subject to superstition, and put a good deal of credence in their dreams and those things which one has a good deal of trouble to wean them from. This episode will be proof of what I say.

This Wolf Indian in his dream imagined that he had only to set out and by dint of travelling would arrive at the celestial dwelling. This he did the next day. Early in the morning he arose and equipped himself for a hunting journey, not forgetting to take provisions and ammunition, and a big kettle. Behold him then setting out like that on his journey to Heaven to see the Master of Life.

The first seven days of his journey were quite favorable to his plans; he walked on without growing discouraged, always with a firm belief that he would arrive at his destination, and eight days went by without his encountering anything which could hinder him in his desire. On the evening of the eighth day he halted at sunset as usual, at the opening to a little prairie upon the bank of a stream which seemed to him a suitable camping place. As he was preparing his shelter for the night he beheld at the other end of this prairie where he camped, three roads, wide and plainly marked. This struck him as singular, nevertheless, he went on working on his shelter so as to be protected from the weather, and made a fire. While doing his cooking he thought he noticed that the three roads became all the brighter the darker it grew, a thing which surprised him to the point of fear. He hesitated for some time over what he should do, whether to remain in his present camp, or move and camp elsewhere; but as he pondered he recalled his incantations, or rather his dream, and that he had undertaken this journey from no other reason than to see the Master of Life. This led him to believe that one of the roads was the one he must take to reach the spot he desired. He concluded to remain where he was till the next day, when he would choose one of the three routes at random. However, his curiosity hardly allowed him time to reflect upon it before he abandoned his camp and set out along the road which seemed to him the widest. He continued in it for half a day without seeing anything to stop him, but, pausing a little to take breath, he saw suddenly a great fire coming out of the earth. This aroused his curiosity. He drew nearer to see what this fire was, but the closer he approached the more the fire appeared to increase. This frightened him and caused him to retrace his steps and take another road which was narrower than the first one.

After following this road the same length of time as the other he beheld the same spectacle, and his fear which had been quieted by the change of route was again aroused. He was once more obliged to turn about and take the third road which he followed for a day without discovering anything. Suddenly he saw before him what appeared to be a mountain of marvellous whiteness and he stopped, overcome with astonishment. Nevertheless, he again advanced, firmly determined to see what this mountain could be, but when he arrived at the foot of it he no longer saw any road and was sad. At this juncture, not knowing what to do to continue his way, he looked around in all directions and finally saw a woman of this mountain, of radiant beauty, whose garments dimmed the whiteness of the snow. And she was seated.

This woman addressed him in his own tongue: "Thou appearest to me surprised not to find any road to lead thee where thou wishest to go. I know that for a long while thou hast been desirous of seeing the Master of Life and of speaking with Him; that is why thou hast undertaken this journey to see Him. The road which leads to His abode is over the mountain, and to ascend it thou must forsake all that thou hast with thee, and disrobe completely, and leave all thy trappings and clothing at the foot of the mountain. No one shall harm thee; go and bathe thyself in a river which I shall show thee, and then thou shalt ascend."

The Wolf was careful to obey the words of the woman, but one difficulty yet confronted him, namely, to know how to reach the top of the mountain which was perpendicular, pathless, and smooth as ice. He questioned this woman how one should go about climbing up, and she replied that if he was really anxious to see the Master of Life he would have to ascend, helping himself only with his hand and his left foot. This appeared to him impossible, but encouraged by the woman he set about it and succeeded by dint of effort.

When he reached the top he was greatly astonished not to see anyone; the woman had disappeared, and he found himself alone without a guide. At his right were three villages which confronted him; he did not know them for they seemed of different construction from his own, prettier and more orderly in appearance. After he had pondered some time over what he ought to do, he set out toward the village which seemed to him the most attractive, and covered half the distance from the top of the mountain before he remembered that he was naked. He was afraid to go farther, but he heard a voice telling him to continue and that he ought not to fear, because, having bathed as he had, he could go on in assurance. He had no more difficulty in continuing up to a spot which seemed to him to be the gate of the village, and here he stopped, waiting for it to open so he could enter. While he was observing the outward beauty of this village the gate opened, and he saw coming toward him a handsome man, clothed all in white, who took him by the hand and told him that he was going to satisfy him and let him talk with the Master of Life. The Wolf permitted the man to conduct him, and both came to a place of surpassing beauty which the Indian could not admire enough. Here he saw the Master of Life, who took him by the hand and gave him a hat all bordered with gold to sit down upon. The Wolf hesitated to do this for fear of spoiling the hat, but he was ordered to do so, and obeyed without reply.

After the Indian was seated the Lord said to him: "I am the Master of Life, and since I know what thou desirest to know, and to whom thou wishest to speak, listen well to what I am going to say to thee and to all the Indians:

"I am He who hath created the heavens and the earth, the trees, lakes, rivers, all men, and all that thou seest and hast seen upon the earth. Because I love you, ye must do what I say and love, and not do what I hate. I do not love that ye should drink to the point of madness, as ye do; and I do not like that ye should fight one another. Ye take two wives, or run after the wives of others; ye do not well, and I hate that. Ye ought to have but one wife, and keep her till death. When ye wish to go to war, ye conjure and resort to the medicine dance, believing that ye speak to me; ye are mistaken,—it is to Manitou that ye speak, an evil spirit who prompts you to nothing but wrong, and who listens to you out of ignorance of me.

"This land where ye dwell I have made for you and not for others. Whence comes it that ye permit the Whites upon your lands? Can ye not live without them? I know that those whom ye call the children of your Great Father supply your needs, but if ye were not evil, as ye are, ye could surely do without them. Ye could live as ye did live before knowing them,—before those whom ye call your brothers had come upon your lands. Did ye not live by the bow and arrow? Ye had no need of gun or powder, or anything else, and nevertheless ye caught animals to live upon and to dress yourselves with their skins. But when I saw that ye were given up to evil, I led the wild animals to the depths of the forests so that ye had to depend upon your brothers to feed and shelter you. Ye have only to become good again and do what I wish, and I will send back the animals for your food. I do not forbid you to permit among you the children of your Father; I love them. They know me and pray to me, and I supply their wants and all they give you. But as to those who come to trouble your lands,—drive them out, make war upon them. I do not love them at all; they know me not, and are my enemies, and the enemies of your brothers. Send them back to the lands which I have created for them and let them stay there. Here is a prayer which I give thee in writing to learn by heart and to teach to the Indians and their children."

The Wolf replied that he did not know how to read. He was told that when he should have returned to earth he would have only to give the prayer to the chief of his village who would read it and teach him and all the Indians to know it by heart; and he must say it night and morning without fail, and do what he had just been told to do; and he was to tell all the Indians for and in the name of the Master of Life:

"Do not drink more than once, or at most twice in a day; have only one wife and do not run after the wives of others nor after the girls; do not fight among yourselves; do not 'make medicine,' but pray, because in 'making medicine' one talks with the evil spirit; drive off your lands those dogs clothed in red who will do you nothing but harm. And when ye shall have need of anything address yourselves to me; and as to your brothers, I shall give to you as to them; do not sell to your brothers what I have put on earth for food. In short, become good and ye shall receive your needs. When ye meet one another exchange greeting and proffer the left hand which is nearest the heart.

"In all things I command thee to repeat every morning and night the prayer which I have given thee."

The Wolf promised to do faithfully what the Master of Life told him, and that he would recommend it well to the Indians, and that the Master of Life would be pleased with them. Then the same man who had led him by the hand came to get him and conducted him to the foot of the mountain where he told him to take his outfit again and return to his village. The Wolf did this, and upon his arrival the members of his tribe and village were greatly surprised, for they did not know what had become of him, and they asked where he had been. As he was enjoined not to speak to anybody before he had talked with the chief of his village, he made a sign with his hand that he had come from on high. Upon entering the village he went straight to the cabin of the chief to whom he gave what had been given to him,—namely, the prayer and the law which the Master of Life had given him.

This adventure was soon noised about among the people of the whole village who came to hear the message of the Master of Life, and then went to carry it to the neighboring villages. The members of these villages came to see the pretended traveller, and the news was spread from village to village and finally reached Pontiac. He believed all this, as we believe an article of faith, and instilled it into the minds of all those in his council. They listened to him as to an oracle, and told him that he had only to speak and they were all ready to do what he demanded of them.

Pontiac, delighted at the success of his harangue, told the Hurons and Potawatomies to return to their villages, and that in four days he would go to the Fort with his young men for the peace-pipe dance, and that while the dancers were engaged some other young men would roam around in the Fort to spy out all that was being done, the number of men the English had in the garrison, the number of traders, and the houses they occupied. All of this happened as he had said.

The first Sunday, or rather Sunday, the first day of May, about three o'clock in the afternoon, as the French were coming out of vespers Pontiac came with forty men that he had chosen and presented himself at the entrance gate. But the Commandant, who had got wind of something in the conduct of the Indians, had ordered the sentinels not to let any come in. This surprised Pontiac. Seeing that they refused admission to him and his whole band who expected to enter as usual, they sent for Mr. La Butte, their interpreter, to say in their behalf to the Commandant that they had come to amuse him and dance the peace-pipe dance.[9] At the request of

[9]French-Canadian custom frequently employed two surnames (sometimes more than two) to designate an individual. The Ottawa interpreter here noted was Pierre Chêne, more commonly called La Butte. But the name Chêne was itself a nickname, the original migrant to America having been Pierre St. Onge *dit* Chêne. For the fuller story of the Chêne family see Louise Rau, "The Chêne family in Detroit," in *Burton Hist. Coll. Leaflet,* IX, 3-16.

Pierre Chêne *dit* La Butte, the Ottawa interpreter, was staunchly loyal to the British cause. A nephew (son of Pierre's sister), Jacques Godfroy, on the contrary, sided with Pontiac with the result (having previously taken the oath of allegiance to the British government) that he was convicted of treason and sentenced to be hung. Pierre La Butte was born at Montreal on July 23, 1698. During

Mr. La Butte they received permission. They took up their position to the number of thirty before the house in which Mr. Campbell lived, the second in command, and began to dance and beat a post, and relate their warlike exploits.[10] And from time to time they leaped about the Commander-in-chief and the accompanying officers who were watching the Indians perform, saying to them in defiance that they had beaten the English at various times and would do so again.

After they had finished talking they demanded bread, tobacco, and beer, which were given

or prior to 1717 he joined his father in Detroit, where he became a merchant and official interpreter to the Ottawa tribe. In 1728 he married Marie, daughter of a Miami woman and Pierre Roy, the latter a friend of Cadillac. Marie died in 1732 and La Butte married (second) Louise Lootman *dit* Barrois. On July 31, 1734 he obtained a grant of land three arpents wide lying west of the fort. At the time of the siege he was living on St. Anne Street in the town, where apparently he continued to reside until his death. His garden and outbuildings figure repeatedly in the contemporary narratives of the siege. La Butte died May 13, 1774 and was buried under the Church, to which he had given a thousand livres in merchandise.

[10]Major Donald Campbell of the Royal American Regiment, who came to Detroit with Robert Rogers in 1760 and served as commandant of the post until the arrival of Major Gladwin, after which Campbell remained as second in command. For his murder on July 4, 1763 by Wasson, chief of the Saginaw band of Chippewas, see *post*, 175–76.

to them. They remained long enough so that the ten others who had the word could note all that was going on in the Fort. And nobody, English or French, mistrusted them, since it is frequently their custom to roam around anywhere unhindered. After these ten had made the round of the Fort and closely examined everything, they came back to join the dancers, and all, as if nothing had happened, went away to their village which was located a little distance above the Fort on the other side of the river in the direction of east northeast, where, according to the orders of Pontiac, the Ottawa chief, all the Indians had encamped the previous Friday.[11]

After their return to the village all the spies reported point by point to their chiefs what they had seen: the movements of the English, and the approximate number of the garrison. Following this report Pontiac sent his messengers to the Hurons and the Potawatomies to inform them by means of wampum belts of what had happened at the fort. Mackatepelecite, the second chief of the Ottawas, and another Indian highly regarded among them, were dispatched to Takay, the chief of the bad Huron band, who received them with enthusiasm and promised that

---

[11]The village was opposite Belle Isle Park, on the site of the subsequent town of Walkerville, now incorporated with the city of Windsor.

he and his village were ready to obey the first demand of their great chief.

Pontiac, wholly occupied with his project and nourishing in his heart a poison which was to be fateful for the English, and perhaps for the French, sent runners the following day, Monday, the 2nd of May, to each of the Huron and Potawatomi villages to discover the real feeling of each of these two nations, for he feared to be crossed in his plans. These emissaries had orders to notify these nations for him that Thursday, the 5th of May, at mid-day, a grand council would be held in the Potawatomi village which was situated between two and three miles below the Fort toward the southwest,[12] and that the three nations should meet there and that no woman should be allowed to attend for fear of betraying their plans.

When the appointed day had come all the Ottawas with Pontiac at their head, and the bad band of the Hurons in charge of Takay, repaired to the Potawatomi village where the expected council was to be held. Care had been taken to send the women out of the village so that they might not hear anything of what should be decided. Pontiac ordered sentinels to be placed around the village in order not to be disturbed

[12]Immediately west of the approach to the Ambassador Bridge. See *ante*, note 1, xliii.

in their council. When all these precautions had been taken each Indian seated himself in the circle according to rank and Pontiac at the head, as great chief of all, began to speak. He said:

"It is important for us, my brothers, that we exterminate from our lands this nation which seeks only to destroy us. You see as well as I that we can no longer supply our needs, as we have done, from our brothers, the French. The English sell us goods twice as dear as the French do, and their goods do not last. Scarcely have we bought a blanket or something else to cover ourselves with before we must think of getting another; and when we wish to set out for our winter camps they do not want to give us any credit as our brothers, the French, do.

"When I go to see the English commander and say to him that some of our comrades are dead, instead of bewailing their death, as our French brothers do, he laughs at me and at you. If I ask anything for our sick, he refuses with the reply that he has no use for us. From all this you can well see that they are seeking our ruin. Therefore, my brothers, we must all swear their destruction and wait no longer. Nothing prevents us; they are few in numbers, and we can accomplish it. All the nations who are our brothers attack them,—why should we not attack? Are we not men like them? Have I not shown you the wampum belts which I received from our Great Father, the Frenchman? He tells us to strike them,—why do we not listen to his words? What do we fear? It is time. Do we fear that our brothers, the French, who are here among us will prevent us? They do not know our plans, and they could not hinder anyway, if they would. You all know as well as I that when the English came upon our lands to drive out our Father, Bellestre[13], they took away all the Frenchmen's guns and that they now have no arms to protect themselves with. Therefore, it is time for us to strike. If there are any French who side with them, let us strike them as well as the English. Remember what the Master of Life told our brother, the Wolf, to do. That concerns us all as

[13]François Marie Picoté, Sieur de Bellestre, was the last French commandant of Detroit, holding this office from 1756 until the place was yielded to Major Robert Rogers, November 29, 1760. Bellestre was a veteran soldier whose military activities carried him widely over the eastern half of North America. In 1747 he was appointed commandant of St. Joseph at present-day Niles, Michigan. It affords a curious illustration of the inconsistencies of fame that although Bellestre had led or shared in repeated raids upon the English settlements, in whose course the settlers were subjected to wholesale massacre, Detroit historians commonly hold him in high regard. (For example Judge Campbell and C. M. Burton.) For officially promoting (although not accompanying) such raids during the American Revolution the name and memory of Lieutenant Governor Henry Hamilton of Detroit are still

well as others. I have sent wampum belts and messengers to our brothers, the Chippewas of Saginaw, and to our brothers, the Ottawas of Michilimackinac, and to those of the Thames River to join us. They will not be slow in coming, but while we wait let us strike anyway. There is no more time to lose. When the English are defeated we shall then see what there is left to do, and we shall stop up the ways hither so that they may never come again upon our lands."

The speech, which Pontiac delivered in such an energetic tone, produced its desired effect upon the members of the council, and they all swore with one accord the complete destruction of the English. It was decided before the council closed that Pontiac at the head of sixty chosen men should go to the Fort to ask the English Commander for a grand council, and that they should have weapons hidden under their blankets, and that the rest of the village, armed with

regarded as infamous. For a fuller sketch of Bellestre's career see article by C. M. Burton in *Michigan Pioneer Colls.*, XXXIV, 336–40. This officer should not be confused with a predecessor of identical name who was stationed at Detroit from about 1721 until his death, October 9, 1729. It was this Bellestre who (through marriage) brought to Detroit the far-flung and still numerous Beaubien line. See *Burton Hist. Coll. Leaflet*, VII, 34 and Father Christian Denissen's compilation of genealogies of families of French Detroit (Ms. in Burton Historical Collection, Detroit Public Library).

tomahawks, dirks, and knives, also hidden under
their blankets, should follow them and enter the
Fort. In order not to arouse any suspicion they
were to stroll about while the former attended
the council with the Commandant. The Ottawa
women were also to enter, furnished with short-
ened guns and other weapons hidden under
their blankets, and take up their position in the
rear streets of the Fort and await the signal,
which should be a war-cry given by the great
chief.[14] All together should fall upon the English, taking good care not to harm the French
who lived in the Fort. The Hurons and the
Potawatomies were to divide into two bands,—
one to go down the river to cut off those who

[14]John Porteous, an intelligent English trader, many
of whose surviving papers are preserved in the Burton
Historical Collection, states that the signal for the attack
was to be given by the way Pontiac turned a belt of wampum (white on one side and green on the other) while in
the act of presenting it to Major Gladwin. Displaying the
belt, white side uppermost, he made a long speech, to be
terminated by the assault which was to begin when he
turned the green side uppermost. Baffled by the readiness
of the garrison for defense, and by the obvious knowledge
that his plot had been discovered, Pontiac did not dare
display the fatal signal. A life-size mural on a wall of the
Detroit Public Library exhibits the artist's conception of
the scene at the moment of presenting the belt to Major
Gladwin. The statement that the signal for the attack was
to be the turning of the belt by Pontiac is repeated by
Thomas Mante in his near-contemporary *History of the
Late War in North America,* published at London in 1772.

should come (from that way),[15] the other to remain around the Fort at a distance to kill those
who were working outside; and in all the villages
the war-song was to be chanted.

After all the plans were made on this day each
nation withdrew to its village, resolved to carry
out the orders of the great chief. But whatever
precautions they took against being discovered,
God brought it about that they were discovered,
as I shall relate.

An Ottawa Indian named Mahiganne, who
had but feebly assented to the conspiracy and
was displeased at the evil behavior of those of his
tribe, came Friday night, unbeknown to the
other Indians, to the gate of the Fort and asked
to speak to the Commandant, saying he had
something of importance to communicate to
him alone. The gate was opened and he was
conducted to Mr. Campbell, second in command, who had Mr. Gladwin, the commander-in-
chief, notified. They wanted to notify Mr. La
Butte, the interpreter, but the Indian did not
wish it, saying that he could speak enough
French to make himself understood by Mr.
Campbell. He then explained to the two commanders the conspiracy of the Indians, and how
they were all evil-disposed and had sworn their

[15]That is, to intercept parties of traders or soldiers
coming from Niagara or other points eastward to Detroit.

destruction and in the course of that very day were to fall upon them, and that they must be on their guard. He also begged the commander not to tell anybody, either of the French or the English, what he had just related to them, because the rest of the Indians would not fail to find it out sooner or later, and knowing about it they would kill him from rage at having failed in their attack. The Commandant thanked him and wanted to reward him with presents. The Indian would not take any and again begged the commanders not to betray him, and the promise was made and kept.[16]

The commanders, after they had heard this report, which appeared to them to be true, gave orders at once that the guard should be doubled at daybreak, and that there should be two sentries at each big gate, and that the two small gates should be closed. This was quickly done.

[16]Numerous versions of the informant who disclosed the plot to Major Gladwin exist, but the secret still remains undisclosed. Perhaps the most popular version identifies the informant as an Indian maiden who was Major Gladwin's mistress. A painting by John M. Mix showing her supposed interview with the Commandant is preserved in the Burton Historical Collection. Pontiac's own identification of Catherine, the Chippewa squaw, as the culprit is related by our Author on a subsequent page. For a discussion of the conflicting versions concerning Gladwin's informant see Peckham, *Pontiac and the Indian Uprising,* Chap. 7.

The officers were also enjoined to inspect the arms of their troops and warn them to be ready to appear at the first roll of the drum. All of this was to be done without any commotion so that the Indians coming into the Fort might not notice that their plans were discovered. The orders were carried out so well that the French did not know anything about it.

May 7.

The fatal day which was the 7th of May and the 26th of the moon, following the Indian custom of reckoning time, having arrived for the English and perhaps for the French, Pontiac, who believed his designs still a secret, ordered in the morning that all his men should chant the war-song and paint themselves and put feathers in their hair,—an Indian custom when about to go on the warpath; moreover, all were to be armed with whatever was necessary for the attack.

Toward ten o'clock in the morning he came in his trappings to ask for a council, and it was granted. All of his men to the number of sixty who were to take part in the council entered the house of Mr. Campbell, second in command, where Mr. Gladwin, commander-in-chief, was with a part of his officers, who were all aware of the bold designs of Pontiac and had arms concealed in their pockets. The rest of the officers were occupied in getting their troops in readi-

AN IDEALIZED VIEW OF FORT DETROIT

Chiefly based on the map drawn by Joseph Gaspard Chaussegros De Lery, a French army engineer, on August 20, 1749.
Courtesy of the Detroit Public Library.

ness to appear when wanted. This was done
with so much dispatch that the Indians did not
have any occasion for suspicion. While the council was assembling, the other Ottawa Indians entered and took their places according to the
plans agreed upon among them.

Pontiac in the council, thinking that it was
about time for all of the people to have entered
and taken positions in readiness for the attack,
went out to see for himself if all his followers
were ready and to give the signal which, as I
have said, was to be a war-whoop. He perceived
some commotion attracting the attention of his
men toward the drill-ground and wanted to see
what it might be. He noticed that the troops
were under arms and drilling. This maneuver
augured ill for the success of his plot, inasmuch
as he was surely discovered and his project defeated. He was disconcerted at this and obliged
to re-enter the council room where all his men
had remained waiting only for the cry to attack.
They were greatly surprised when they saw him
come back; they suspected that they were discovered and that, since they could no longer succeed, for the present they must leave and put off
the attack to another day. They talked it over
among themselves for some time, and then without saying good bye or anything they went out of
the gate to regain their village where they might

take other measures against discovery and succeed better.

Pontiac, upon his return to the village, found
himself overwhelmed by various emotions,—
anger, fury, and rage. As one might have thought,
he looked like a lioness robbed of all her whelps.
He assembled all his young men and made in-
quiries among them to see if they did not know
the one that had betrayed them, "because," he
said to them, "I see very well that the English
have been warned." He gave them orders to
try to find out the traitor in the nation, for
they must kill him. But all their efforts were
in vain; the one who had informed against them
had taken too many precautions for them to
discover him.

In the meantime, toward four o'clock in the
afternoon there arrived in the village a false
rumor that it was a Chippewa woman who had
betrayed them, and that she was concealed in
the Potawatomi village. At this report Pontiac
ordered four Indians to find her and bring her
to him, and these, taking delight naturally in
lawlessness, were not so slow to do what their
chief told them. They crossed the river directly
in front of the village and passed by the Fort,
quite naked but for breechclouts, with knives
in their hands. They were yelling as they went
along that their plan had failed, which caused

the French along the shore, who knew nothing about the plot of the Indians, to think they had some evil designs either upon them or upon the English. They arrived at the Potawatomi village and actually found the woman, who had not even thought of them. Nevertheless, they took her and made her walk ahead of them, all the while uttering yells of joy as if they had a victim upon whom they were going to vent their cruelty. They took her into the Fort and before the Commandant as if to confront her with him, and demand if she was not the one who had disclosed to him their plans. They got no more satisfaction than if they had kept quiet; the Commandant ordered bread and beer for them and for her, and then they took her to their chief in their village.[17]

It was now a question in the village of inventing some ruse to conceal their treachery and

[17]Poor Catherine, who is variously described and identified in the several contemporary and old-age narratives of the siege, was given a beating by Pontiac, after which, save for one old-age recollection, she disappears from recorded history. Henry Connor, son of the first permanent white settler of St. Clair County, and himself an interpreter at Detroit in the early nineteenth century, related that he was acquainted with Catherine; that she was young (in 1763) and in love with Gladwin; and that she unromantically perished long afterward by falling while drunk into a vat of boiling maple syrup. See Peckham, *Pontiac and the Indian Uprising*, 122–23, 132–33.

carry through their evil projects. Pontiac, whose genius constantly supplied him with new resources, said that he had thought out another scheme which would succeed better than the first one, and that the next day he would act upon it; he would go to speak with the Commandant to try to undeceive him concerning what had been told him, and he would play his part so well with these gentlemen in disproving the falsehood, that as soon as they heard him they would fall into his trap and he could accomplish his purpose before they knew it.

Fortunately, however, the Commandant and all the officers who had escaped the danger which threatened them and were safe only as long as they were on their guard, were not the kind of men to be caught by the flattering talk of a traitor; consequently, all that the enmity of Pontiac could devise against them was useless. But still he attempted to come to the Fort, as if sure of his plan, and actually did come as he had told his followers he would do.

May 8th, Sunday,

About one o'clock in the afternoon he came, accompanied by Mackatepelicite, Breton, and Chavinon, all chiefs of the same Ottawa nation. They brought with them a calumet, which they call among themselves the calumet of peace. They asked and were granted an audience by the

Commandant, and did all they could with fine words to deceive him and lead him and all his troops into the snare which they had set for him. Warned of their wicked intrigues the Commandant acted as if he believed what they told him, but nevertheless was on his guard.

Pontiac told him, as proof of his cherishing no bad designs, that he had brought the pipe of peace for them to smoke together in token of agreement; and that he was going to leave it with him as a guarantee of the Indians' uprightness, and that as long as he had it he need not fear anything from them. The Commandant accepted the pipe, which he well knew was a feeble guarantee against the bad faith of an Indian. After the Commandant had received it Pontiac withdrew with his chiefs, well satisfied and believing that his tricks had succeeded and entangled the English in the snares which his wickedness had set for them. But without knowing it he was deceived in his expectations.

He and his chiefs returned to his village as happy as if they were sure of the success of their enterprise, and in a few words they reported to their young men the result of their negotiations. They sent messengers to the bad band of the Hurons and to the Potawatomies to notify them of what they had just accomplished at the Fort, and that the next day was the one which should settle the fate of these Englishmen, and that they should hold themselves ready for the first call.

In order to play his part better and make it appear that neither he nor his followers cherished evil designs any longer, Pontiac invited for four o'clock in the afternoon the good and bad Huron bands and the Potawatomies to come and play lacrosse with his young men.[18] A good many French from each side of the river came to play also, and were well received by the three nations. The game lasted till about seven o'clock in the evening, and when it was over everybody thought of returning home. The French who lived on the Fort side of the river and had been beaten were obliged to recross the river in order to return

[18]The game of lacrosse was a favorite diversion among the Algonquin tribes of mid-America. One of the most spirited descriptions of their addiction to it was penned by a young Frenchman in the Illinois country in the closing years of the seventeenth century. See the De Gannes Memoir, in *Illinois Hist. Colls.* XXIII, 342–43. The present-day city of Lacrosse, Wisconsin, derives its name from the fact that its site was a favorite resort of the Sioux, and possibly other tribes, for indulging in the game. In the excitement of the contest the players risked life and limb more recklessly than do present-day members of professional hockey or football teams. The fall of Mackinac on June 2, 1763 was accomplished by the trick of staging a game of lacrosse adjoining the fort, into which the warriors rushed in ostensible pursuit of the ball, which had purposely been batted into it.

home. As they embarked in their canoes they began to utter warwhoops and yells of victory, as the Indians do when they have won a game. The officers in command, ever on the alert, thought it was the Indians crossing to fall upon the Fort and massacre them; they ordered the gates to be closed quickly and the troops and traders to take up their positions on the ramparts for defense in case of attack. However, it was only a false alarm occasioned by the imprudence of the young Frenchmen who did not realize the situation.

Pontiac, who had no thought whatever of coming to the Fort, was for the moment occupied with the Hurons and the Potawatomies who had remained in the village. After the game he related to them all the details of the parley between the commanders and himself and his chiefs, telling them that according to the word of these gentlemen he was to return the following day to smoke the pipe of peace, or rather of treason, and that he hoped to succeed.

But he reckoned without his host.

May 9, Monday; The First day of Rogations.[19]

---

[19]Rogation days are the three days preceding Ascension Day. In the Roman Catholic Church the litany of the saints is chanted in procession on each of the three days.

Following the custom of the church the curate and all the clergy conducted the procession outside the Fort without incurring any harm. Likewise mass was celebrated, after which everybody in his own house wondered how the day would pass, knowing full well that Pontiac would make some other attempt.

The good people secretly lamented the evil fate which threatened the English, who did not have much of a force. Their garrison consisted of about one hundred and thirty troops, including the officers, eight in number, and some forty men, traders and their employees. In addition, they had two vessels of unequal size which were anchored in front of the Fort and defended the place from the side toward the river.[20] They

---

[20]Although Cadillac, with his customary far-sightedness had advocated the development of a fleet of sailing vessels on the Upper Lakes, to the end of the French regime none were built, save for La Salle's ill-fated *Griffon* in 1679 and a twenty-five ton vessel built by the Sieur de la Ronde (about 1734) for service on Lake Superior. Following the surrender of Canada to the English in 1760, the newcomers moved swiftly to develop a naval fleet on the upper Lakes. A navy yard was established at Niagara (hence the name of Navy Island), where the schooner *Huron* was launched in 1761. In 1762 the sloop *Michigan* was completed and both vessels played an essential role in the defense of Detroit in 1763. In the papers of Parkman the *Huron* and the *Michigan* are mistakenly named the *Beaver* and the *Gladwin*. For their story see M. M. Quaife, "The Royal Navy of the Upper Lakes," in *Burton Hist. Coll. Leaflet*, II, 49–64.

would have been too few if the Indians by any chance had been good soldiers.[21]

Pontiac, who had concealed in his breast the murderous knife which was to cut short the life of these people, set out to go to the Fort with fifty men of his nation in accordance with what he had arranged the night before with the Hurons. The others were to observe the same behavior as on the preceding Saturday.

About eleven o'clock he presented himself at the gates with his followers, but he was refused admission in pursuance of an order of the Commandant. He insisted upon entering, asking to speak to the Commandant, and saying that he and his chiefs had come only to smoke the pipe of peace in accordance with the promise which the Commandant had given them. He was told that he could easily enter, but only with twelve or fifteen of the leading men of his nation and no more. He replied that all his people wanted to smell the smoke of the peace-pipe, and that if they could not enter he would not enter either.

[21]Uncertainty prevails concerning the actual strength of the garrison. It comprised two companies of the Royal American Regiment and one of the Queen's Rangers, plus the crews of the *Huron* and the *Michigan*. Peckham concludes that the force available at the opening of hostilities may have numbered 120 soldiers, in addition to which there were some 20 or more English traders whose assistance could be counted upon. See *Pontiac and the Indian Uprising*, 127–28.

He was promptly refused and was forced to return to his village in a bad humor. However, this disturbed these gentlemen very little. The Commandant had the French warned to keep in their houses.

Pontiac, enraged to see that his last stratagem had failed and all his projects were wrecked, caught up a tomahawk as soon as he entered his village and chanted the war-song, saying that inasmuch as he could not strike the English within the Fort he would attack those on the outside; he ordered all his people, men, women, and children, to cross the river to the side where the Fort was, in order to harass it the better, and pitch camp on the shore at Baptiste Meloche's, a mile and a quarter above the Fort.[22] This was done promptly.

He divided his men into several bands to attack in different places; one band went half a mile back

[22]Actually about twice this distance.

The Detroit Meloches were descended from François Meloche and Mary Blouin, who lived in the town of Cogne, France. Their son François, born there, married at Montreal, Oct. 25, 1700, Marie Mouflet, a native of Lachine. Their son, Pierre, born Sept. 1, 1701, married Jane Caron at Lachine, August 16, 1724. Soon thereafter the young couple came to Detroit and settled on a farm east of the fort (the present-day George Hunt Farm, Private Claim No. 182) adjoining Parent's Creek. Here Jean Baptiste, our present subject, was born, Feb. 19, 1741. On Nov. 11, 1760 he married Marie Louise Robert. He obtained

from the Fort, where an old English woman lived
with her two sons who cultivated for themselves
seven or eight acres of land and kept a good deal
of cattle, such as oxen and cows. These poor
people, suspecting nothing, were killed, scalped,
their property plundered, and their house set on
fire.[23] It was a terrible spectacle to see how the
fire took sides with the Indians; the dead bodies
were burned up in the house. The Indians
killed a part of the cattle and drove off the
rest, some of which escaped into the woods
and were later found by the French settlers
along the coasts.

title to his father's farm on which he passed his entire
life. He operated a grist mill on Parent's Creek, since
1763 better known as Bloody Run, where Captain Dalyell
was defeated in the night of July 31. Of this affair Mrs.
Meloche dictated an old-age account which is published
in *Mich. Pioneer Colls.*, VIII, 340–44. Jean Baptiste and
his wife were the parents of eight children. He was buried Sept. 16, 1820; Mrs. Meloche was living as late as
1824. See Denissen, Detroit Genealogies (ms.) and *Mich.
Pioneer Colls.*, VIII, 348.

[23]The obscure victims of this initial atrocity were a
Mrs. Turnbull and her two sons. Conceivably she may
have been the widow of a deceased or discharged British
soldier, or the victim, with her sons, of some Indian
raiding party which had carried them as captives to
Detroit. James H. Lanman, whose history of Michigan
was published in 1839, affirms that the Indians ate Mrs.
Turnbull's body. Gabriel St. Aubin's old-age narrative
discloses that as late as 1824 the site of the Turnbull
home was known as *Le champ-de-la-vielle*—Old Woman's
field. See *Mich. Pioneer Colls.*, VIII, 352.

While this first band were engaged in their work of carnage, the other band went to Hog Island[24] where there lived a man named Fisher, a former sergeant of the English army. This man with his family of five or six persons was working for half the profit a little farm which the English officers had appropriated for themselves. These good people, thinking of nothing but their work, became at a moment when they least expected it victims of the fury of the Indians, who fell upon the man and scalped him; they wanted to carry his wife away prisoner because she was pretty, but she would not go, saying that since her husband was dead she wished to die with him. They killed her and her woman servant, and carried off the two little children to their village to be slaves[25].

---

[24]Following the founding of Detroit, Belle Isle (now a city park) was set aside as a common for the use of all the settlers. It was utilized to pasture their domestic animals and probably for this reason was named *Ile au Cochon*, or Hog Island. The present name of Belle Isle was acquired toward the middle of the nineteenth century, given, according to one account, in honor of the daughter of Governor Cass. A popular legend to the effect that the name Hog Island was given because the settlers populated it with hogs to destroy the rattlesnakes which abounded there has no historical validity.

[25]James Fisher, a retired sergeant in the army, and his family may perhaps be deemed the first permanent residents of Belle Isle. Varying accounts are given of the number of English persons on the Island at the time of the massacre. In addition to Fisher, his wife and his two

A Frenchman by the name of Goslin who was working on the island squaring building timbers had not been informed of what was about to

children, there were several other adults (English) and one Frenchman, François Goslin, whose fate is narrated by our author. The number of victims slain was six—Mr. and Mrs. Fisher, their domestic servant, two soldiers, and Goslin. Contemporary accounts indicate that three, rather than two, Fisher children may have been taken prisoners. One child is reported to have been taken to Saginaw. *Mich. Pioneer Colls.*, VIII, 352. Another, 15-months-old Marie, died in the Fort in October. Betty Fisher was carried to the Maumee River, where she was shockingly murdered in 1764.

From the massacre of the Fisher household a characteristic folk-tale developed. Jacques Amable Peltier, a boy of sixteen in 1763, in 1824 related that his father and some other Frenchmen went to the Island the day after the massacre to bury the victims. Mr. and Mrs. Fisher were interred in a common grave. The next day the burial party again visited the Island, when the hand of Fisher was found sticking out above the grave. They reburied it, only to find the phenomenon repeated a few days later. They now related the affair to Father Bocquet, who visited the scene and recited some prayers over the grave, with the result that dead Fisher's hand ceased to extrude from the grave.

One further horror tale developed from the Fisher massacre. Following the war Jean Maiet accused Alexis Cuillerier of drowning seven-year-old Betty Fisher. Cuillerier fled from Detroit because of his part in the war, but following its close he was apprehended and placed on trial for murder by Captain Turnbull, the new commandant of Detroit. Although he fled from custody, the testimony of Pontiac and others seems clearly to establish his guilt. For the detailed story of the crime see Peckham, *Pontiac and the Indian Uprising*, 301–303.

happen to Fisher. Upon hearing the cries of the
Indians as they landed on the island, he thought
to save himself from the danger which seemed
to threaten him as much as the English: he
was caught upon the beach by the Indians who
put him in a canoe and told him to stay there,
saying that he had nothing to fear for himself
as they did not intend to do him any harm.
He did not believe it nor want to stay where
they had put him. His unbelief cost him dear,
for, upon trying to escape into the depths of the
island, the Indians took him for some fleeing
Englishman; they ran after him and killed him,
and when they were upon the point of scalping
him they recognized that it was a Frenchman.
They placed him in their canoe and gave him
to the French who buried him in the cemetery.

About four o'clock in the afternoon an inhabitant of the East Coast, Mr. Desnoyers[26], who
had gone to the pine woods sixty miles above

[26]Several lines of Desnoyers were represented in early
Detroit. The individual here noted was Pierre Desnoyers,
a native of Lower Canada, whose marriage in Detroit in
1754 is recorded in the St. Anne Parrish Register. He was
a master carpenter who lived on the south side of the
Detroit River (vicinity of modern Sandwich). He was
buried at Assumption Church, Sandwich, August 26,
1776. See Denissen, Detroit Genealogies (Ms.)

The "pine woods" or the "Pinery" on Pine River in St.
Clair County was for several generations Detroit's chief
source of pine timber.

the fort to fell building timber, returned with the Chippewas of Saginaw who escorted him. Through him one learned of the death of two officers, one of whom was Mr. Robertson, ship captain, the other a Sir Knight and colonel of militia. These two gentlemen, acting under orders of the Commandant, had gone with ten soldiers and a Pawnee servant to sound the channels to see if there was enough water for a vessel to pass in case of need[27]. When they left the Fort they

[27]A necessary consequence of the introduction of sailing vessels on the Upper Lakes was the exploration and charting of their waters. As early as the summer of 1761 Sir William Johnson, en route to an Indian council at Detroit, paid a visit to the Navy Island shipyard "whereon the vessel is building for exploring Lakes Huron and Michigan." A few weeks later, returning from Detroit, he found the ship (the schooner *Huron*) had been launched and Lieutenant Charles Robertson was engaged in sounding the Niagara near the entrance to Lake Erie. In 1762 and again in 1763 Robertson continued the work of exploration, operating from Detroit. Here he passed the winter of 1762–63, and from here on May 2 departed in a large bateau to explore and sound the St. Clair River, since Major Gladwin was eager to learn whether communication with Mackinac by sailing ship was possible. Robertson's party numbered 2 sailors, 6 soldiers, the tourist, Sir Robert Davers, and his "pani," an Indian slave boy, and youthful John Rutherfurd, nephew of Captain Walter Rutherfurd, Trader James Sterling's partner. At a point near the entrance to Lake Huron the party was waylaid and all of its members either killed or made captive. For a detailed account of the affair see Rutherfurd's Journal of a Captivity, *post*.

had heard nothing about the wicked designs of
the Indians and they travelled peacefully along,
thinking themselves quite safe. As they were
passing to the right of the pine woods the
Frenchmen who were working there and had
been warned of the evil intentions of the Indians
toward the English called to them to put them
on their guard. They turned in but would not
believe what the French told them, saying that
when they left the Fort everything was quiet.
The Frenchmen warned them again and again
and advised them not to go farther, as the Indians
would prevent them, and they would better return to the Fort, but they would not listen to
the warnings and went on their way. They encountered some Indians encamped upon a point
at the edge of the river, and these seeing them
pass called to them and showed them some
meat and other supplies to entice them. Still
they would not halt there and this offended the
Indians who pursued and killed them, with the
exception of a young man fifteen or sixteen years
old and the Pawnee, whom they took to make
slaves of.

The two Ottawa bands who had made the attack in the two places I have described, acting
under the orders of Pontiac, their chief, came
back to camp after their exploit and related with
gusto all the circumstances of their cruel ex-

pedition, among other things the death of Goslin whom they had killed by mistake,—a thing that saddened them for some time.

After hearing this story from his young men, Pontiac called all of his followers together before him in order to take new measures to approach the Fort and attack it without risk to them. This was not very difficult to do, seeing that there were several barns and stables sixty-five yards to the rear of the Fort; they belonged to several private individuals who lived in the Fort.

To the northeast, at the right of the gate, about a hundred feet away, was a big garden with the gardener's house,—the whole property belonging to Mr. La Butte, the interpreter. All these buildings were so many entrenchments in the shelter of which the Indians could approach the Fort without any danger; they had discovered this and had made use of the buildings for some time to annoy the Fort. After these new measures were taken the Indians rested, waiting for the next day in order to begin their attack in a new way.

While the Indians were making their arrangements to harass the Fort, the Commandant ordered the two gates at each end to be closed, not to be opened again till the end of this war, but the one which faced the southwest was opened twice more to permit the cows which belonged to the inhabitants of the Fort to enter, and then it was also closed. The only one left was the one facing the river which was opened from time to time for the public needs, because it was guarded by the sloops, which the Indians feared greatly.

Toward six o'clock in the evening Mr. La Butte went out several times by order of the Commandant to placate the Indians and try to pump their secrets out of them. But the Indians, and Pontiac in particular, grew tired of his visits and told him to go back to the Fort and stay there or they would all fall upon him. Seeing that nothing could be gained he went back to the Fort, letting the English hope that the Indians would be more easy to deal with the next day.

In the evening at general orders the Commandant announced that all the English in the Fort, traders and soldiers, should relieve one another at guard duty every six hours on the ramparts all night so as not to be surprised in case of attack at daybreak, which is the hour the Indians usually attack when they are carrying on war. The Commandant himself set the example and spent the night standing sentinel with his officers upon the battery.

May 10. Tuesday.

Following the Commandant's orders the gates remained closed. The Ottawas, who believed that they had only to assail the Fort and the English would surrender at their discretion, opened a very violent fire about four o'clock and made the circuit of the Fort as if they wanted to assault it. This frightened the English a little, who were not as yet accustomed to the maneuvers of the Indians and had had no time to make any preparations for defense. There were, however, in the Fort three pieces of cannon,— two six-pounders and one three-pounder, also three small mortars which were placed over the gate and were as good as useless. The three-pounder was mounted upon the battery which faced the forest in the rear of the Fort and was almost masked by the buildings beyond; the other two pieces were upon the drill-ground and of no value, since there was no suitable place to mount them for firing. There were in addition only the two sloops which could fire, and these at the most protected only the river front, which the Indians were careful not to approach; they kept themselves constantly behind the Fort under cover of the buildings and in the clearing of a hill which commanded the Fort, and at the bottom of which the Fort was built, so that the place was defended rather by the courage and intrepidity of the besieged than vanquished by the besiegers who kept up their fire only until about ten o'clock.[28] They were content to shoot from a distance because they had not much ammunition, hoping when they had got hold of some to begin the onslaught again.

The Commandant, seeing that the fire of the Indians had nearly ceased, ordered Mr. La Butte to go out and talk to them. Mr. Chapoton[29], who lived in the Fort, joined Mr. La Butte to go to the camp of the Indians. With the Commandant's

[28]The original town of Detroit was located close to the river upon a sloping hillside which rose gradually in the rear to a height of perhaps forty feet. In the rear of the stockaded enclosure the ground descended to the Savoyard River (converted in the 1830's into an underground sewer), beyond which it again sloped upward to the vicinity of present-day Fort Street. Because of this terrain an observer on the Canadian shore could view almost the entire interior of the fort, a marked disadvantage from the viewpoint of its defenders. An additional disadvantage, noted here and elsewhere by our Author, was the fact that the elevation in the rear commanded the fort. At the time of the Fox siege of 1712 the invaders were encamped across the Savoyard, where now the great office and banking structures—Federal Reserve Bank, Penobscot Building, Manufacturers Bank, Federal Building, etc. are located. In 1779–80, anticipating the arrival of George Rogers Clark from Kentucky, bringing artillery which would command the Fort, the occupants hurriedly erected the new Fort Lernoult on the height at present-day Fort Street.

[29]Jean Chapoton was born in 1694 in the city of Bagnolles, province of Languedoc, in southern France. He became a surgeon in the French army and in 1719 was

permission several other residents of the Fort seized this occasion to retire to the settlers along the shores, giving as an excuse that they did not want to witness the death of the English.

La Butte and Chapoton set out and on the way took Jacques Godfroy[30] who did not object to going with them inasmuch as it was for the security of the public, hoping that three persons whom the Indians knew and loved would placate them the more easily. The latter two of these

sent to Detroit as surgeon to the garrison. On July 16, 1720 he married Marie Magdelene Esteve, who was born in 1704, and they became the parents of twenty children. She was buried on July 7, 1753; Dr. Chapoton was buried Nov. 12, 1760. In 1734 he was granted a tract of land east of the town extending westward from present-day Hastings Street, and now known as the Charles Moran farm or Private Claim No. 5. As Detroit's only physician for many years, Chapoton served both civilian and military population.

His eldest son and our present subject, Jean Baptiste Chapoton was born on June 17, 1721. On Sept. 10, 1749 he married Elizabeth Godfroy, who died in consequence of her first childbirth, July 25, 1750. Five years later (Sept. 22, 1755) Chapoton married Felicity Cesire. In July, 1763, he was a captain of militia and a man of local influence. He was buried Jan. 22, 1803; his wife, Felicity, was buried on June 7, 1809. They left numerous descendants and the Chapoton family still remains one of the oldest in the Detroit River area. Data adapted from Denissen, Detroit genealogies (Ms.); see also Fannie Anderson, *Doctors Under Three Flags* (Detroit, 1951), 17–18.

[30]Godfroy and Chapoton were brothers-in-law, Godfroy having married Louise Chapoton, sister of Jean Baptiste,

three gentlemen talked with the Indians without showing that they represented the interests of the English. They were listened to very well, or well, at least, to all appearances, which led Mr. La Butte to believe that all would turn out right. Leaving Messrs. Godfroy and Chapoton with the Indians, he returned to the Fort to tell the Commandant that matters were going well and that he had left Godfroy and Chapoton to continue the parley. He hoped that the English would get out of the difficulty at the cost of some presents. Mr. La Butte thought he knew the Indian mind and did not perceive that he was mistaken in his expectations, and that the Indians, Pontiac in particular, knew how to conceal their real intentions with fine words.

Mr. Campbell, second in command, who desired and loved nothing so much as peace and concord, begged Mr. La Butte in the name of Mr. Gladwin,

Jan. 23, 1758. Godfroy was a trader and an interpreter who both before and after his union with Louise Chapoton lived with Indian wives. During the uprising of 1763 he sided openly with the Indians, whom he aided in the capture of Fort Miami at present-day Fort Wayne, Indiana. He was convicted of treason and sentenced to be hung, but was pardoned by General Bradstreet on condition that he conduct Captain Thomas Morris safely to the Illinois country. He subsequently lived down his sad reputation and became one of Detroit's prominent citizens. He was buried June 29, 1795, on the eve of the American occupation of Detroit. Data adapted from Denissen, Detroit Genealogies (Ms.); *The John Askin Papers*, I, 63.

the commander-in-chief, to be good enough to return to Pontiac's camp to help Messrs. Godfroy and Chapoton complete their work of quenching the fires of sedition and the re-establishment of peace between the two parties. Mr. La Butte promised to do whatever he could, and returned to the camp where he found Chapoton and Godfroy, who had not quitted Pontiac through hope of winning him over. Mr. La Butte joined them to do what the commanders had urged him.

Pontiac, shrewd and deceitful, appeared to acquiesce in what these three gentlemen asked of him, and to convey the impression that he consented to peace and union he sent Mr. La Butte and some Indians to the Fort to speak as his representatives to the commanders. This he did to get rid of Mr. La Butte, whom he was beginning to suspect.

The Indians to the number of six or seven entered the Fort with Mr. La Butte. They saluted the commanders and the officers, who shook hands with them in welcome. The Indians spoke in the name of their chief and were heard; they in turn seemed to listen to what the commanders said to them through Mr. La Butte. After some minutes of conversation they asked for bread, and were given as much as they could carry away.

While the Indians were parleying within the Fort, someone started a rumor that Col. Bouquet[31] was about to arrive with two thousand troops. At this false news the Indians, without concluding anything, asked permission to withdraw to carry this information to their chief. The gate was opened for them and they returned alone to their camp and related the news to Pontiac, who instead of being astonished said very plainly that the English had lied and had started the rumor merely to frighten them. He had Messrs. Godfroy and Chapoton retire from the camp for some time, telling them that he would call them after he had spoken to his people about what they had come to say to him. He did this in order to have a chance to ponder at his leisure over some other wicked design.

About five o'clock in the afternoon Pontiac

[31]Lieutenant Colonel Henry Bouquet was a native of Switzerland and a life-long professional soldier of much ability. In 1756 he came to America to assume the rank of lieutenant-colonel in the new Royal American Regiment. Promoted to the rank of colonel in 1758, he served with distinction in the campaign of General Forbes against Fort Duquesne (present-day Pittsburgh). In 1763 he led a small army of Royal Americans and Highlanders again to Fort Pitt, roundly defeating the Indians in the battle of Bushy Run (August 6, 1763) by methods "incomparably" in advance of current military practices. In 1764 he led another army into Ohio, where he compelled the surrender of all prisoners held captive by the Indians and concluded a general peace. He died prematurely (aged forty-six) of a fever at Pensacola, Sept. 2, 1765. See *Dict. Am. Biog.*

summoned Messrs. Godfroy and Chapoton and several other Frenchmen to his camp to tell them that he had mollified his young men and that they would consent to a peace, but in order to conclude it properly they would feel flattered to speak with Mr. Campbell, second in command, in his camp, because they had known him for three years in command at the fort and regarded him as their brother. Nevertheless the savage had concealed in his breast a dagger which was destined to be fateful to this honest man.

The Frenchmen, who did not know what Pontiac had in his mind and believed that he spoke frankly, told him they would willingly do their best to bring Mr. Campbell there if he would agree to let him return without insult when they should have completed their parley. He promised this,—it did not cost him anything to promise! And in order the better to cover his wickedness he ordered the pipe of peace brought to them as a guaranty of what he and his people said to them. The French, particularly Messrs. Godfroy and Chapoton, allowed themselves to be caught in the trap which Pontiac set for them as well as for the English.

While the Indians were concocting this new plot, a Frenchman named Mr. Gouin who had accidentally divined what was in the minds of the Indians because of several interviews with Pontiac in which he had not detected anything favorable to the English, and who had some presentiment of what was going to happen to Mr. Campbell, begged a Frenchman passing by his house to go to the Fort and warn Mr. Campbell of what was brewing at the camp and ask him not to leave the Fort nor trust in the fine words of a treacherous savage.[32]

In the meantime the Frenchmen started on the way back to the Fort, thinking that the mere presence of Mr. Campbell would be sufficient to placate the Indians. Mr. Gouin, who saw them coming from afar, and fearing that a first warning would not be enough, begged Mr. Moran, to whom he explained the situation in a few words, to run and again warn these gentlemen not to go out. Mr. Moran did this. He came in all haste to the Fort to inform these gentlemen in detail of all that Mr. Gouin had told him, and he implored Mr. Campbell with tears in his eyes not to leave,

[32]Captain Campbell's would-be saviour was Claude Jean Thomas Gouin, who came to Detroit from Lower Canada prior to 1742. He married here, Jan. 13, 1742, Mary Joseph Cuillerier *dit* Beaubien. He was a surveyor, who settled on Detroit's Northeast Coast. He was buried at Detroit, May 29, 1776. In 1824 his son Charles, who as a small boy in 1763 witnessed many of the scenes attending the siege, related his recollections of it. Although inaccurate in certain details, the story amply supports our Author's account of Gouin's efforts to save Captain Campbell. For it see *Mich. Pioneer Colls.*, VIII, 344–51.

saying if he went to the camp he would never return.[33]

In the meantime Messrs. Godfroy and Chapoton
arrived at the Fort with several Frenchmen with
them, and related to the English the fine words
of Pontiac and showed the pipe of peace which
they had brought. The pipe and the fine words
made upon them all the impression which Pontiac had promised himself, and the two warnings of Mr. Gouin were rendered useless. After-

---

[33]Claude Charles Moran was the founder of the still-
flourishing Detroit line of Morans. He was born at Quebec
on June 18, 1722 and migrated to Detroit prior to September 22, 1751, on which date he married Marie Anne
Belleperche. In or prior to 1758 he acquired a land
grant three arpents wide on the south (Canadian) side
of the river a short distance below present-day Sandwich.
On August 25, 1761 he exchanged this tract for another
lying east of the fort at Hastings Street, now known as
Private Claim No. 5 or the Charles Moran farm. He
subsequently (in 1773) acquired the adjoining land on
the east (Private Claim No. 6 or the Louis Moran farm)
giving him a holding four arpents wide, bisected by
Hastings Street, and one of the choicest farms on the
Detroit River. Additional property came to him and he
remained a leading citizen of the community until his
tragic death by stabbing at the hands of his brother-
in-law, John Joseph Hacker, on December 9, 1775. The
murder precipitated a governmental crisis which constitutes an important chapter in the history of revolu-
tionary Detroit. Hacker was publicly hung on the Detroit
Common in the same month of December, 1775. Data
adapted from J. Bell Moran, The *Moran Family. 200
years in Detroit* (Detroit, 1949), Chaps. II and III.

ward the English wished they had listened to the opinions of others, but it was too late.

Mr. Campbell, who was of a character which desired only unity and concord, believed that he had only to present himself at the camp to allay the storm, and that his presence for a moment would be more than sufficient to bring about peace between the two parties. This, added to the urging of Messrs. Godfroy and Chapoton who said to him that they would answer for him with their lives, caused him to hesitate no longer. He set out, accompanied by Mr. McDougall[34], officer of troops, Mr. La Butte, and a large number of French from the Fort who followed them in the belief that the presence merely of this perfectly upright man would bring about the end of the

---

[34]Lieutenant George McDougall came to Detroit in 1761, where he presently established a local status by marrying (in 1763) Marie Françoise Navarre, daughter of Robert Navarre, the royal notary. In 1762 McDougall built a house on Belle Isle, cleared some land, and established a tenant there. Following the close of the war he continued to claim title to the Island and in 1768 purchased it from the Ottawas and Chippewas for five barrels of rum and a variety of other merchandise. Since it had long been a part of the French Common the inhabitants made a vigorous protest against McDougall's pretensions, despite which he obtained a grant of the island from the King. For details of the complex controversy over the title to it see C. M. Burton, *The City of Detroit, Michigan* 1701–1922, I, 438–62. Eventually (in 1879) the City purchased the Island from its owners

plot; and after his return which ought to follow, so to speak, at once after the conclusion of the council they would be at liberty to go about their business affairs. But they were disappointed in their expectations. Mr. Campbell arrived at the camp where the Indians, as soon as they saw him coming, made the air resound with the most horrible yells. Pontiac had to make use of all his authority to silence them.

Pontiac went to meet Mr. Campbell, took him by the hand and greeted him. To conceal his duplicity the better he asked him to be seated near him, adding that he was delighted to see him for he esteemed him like a Frenchman, and he and his followers were going to open negotiations.[35]

for $200,000. Lieutenant McDougall remained at Detroit until 1778 when as a Captain in the Eighty-fourth Regiment he was transferred to Carleton Island. In 1780, beset by illness, he sold his commission on April 8 and died (in Montreal) the same day. Besides his widow, he left two sons, George (born June 30, 1764) and Robert (born Oct. 19, 1766) to carry on the family name and activities.

[35]The council to which Campbell had been summoned by Pontiac took place in the house of Antoine Cuillerier, brother-in-law of Bellestre, the late French commandant of Detroit, and father of Angelique Cuillerier, one of the reputed informants of Pontiac's plot against the garrison. In a court of inquiry proceedings convened by Major Gladwin on August 9, 1763 Lieutenant McDougall testified that Cuillerier seated himself in the middle of the

For a good hour Mr. Campbell and his officers sat there without the Indians speaking of anything, from which he began to draw an evil augury for his errand. He remarked this to the Frenchmen who had brought him, and they replied that according to the promise of Pontiac he would be free to return whenever he wished. He already wanted to do this. Beginning to feel annoyed, he had Pontiac informed that since there was nothing to talk over he was going to go back. Pontiac, who feared to let slip such a prey and who believed that by holding these two officers in his camp the others would come to his terms, replied that after these two gentlemen had passed two nights with him he would send them back to the Fort. Thus it came that these men handed themselves over as prisoners to the Indians. The Frenchmen of the Fort who had accompanied them returned sadder

largest room in the house with a laced hat and coat on. He kept both his seat and his hat on when Captain Campbell entered, and during the ensuing proceedings Pontiac informed Cuillerier that he regarded him as the Commandant of Detroit until Bellestre should return. Pontiac further informed Captain Campbell and Lieutenant McDougall that if peace were to be concluded the terms would be the same as the English had accorded Bellestre in 1760: they must surrender their arms and baggage and be conducted away by an escort of savages. McDougall's further testimony indicated that Cuillerier conducted himself in every respect as a full-fledged ally of Pontiac. For the proceedings see *Michigan Pioneer Colls.,* XXVII, 639–43.

than when they had set out, for they knew very well that it was a subterfuge by which Pontiac and his followers hoped to circumvent the people of the Fort. When they reached the Fort they recounted to Mr. Gladwin all that had happened at the camp and how his men were detained,—all of which gave him occasion to think that he would have done better to trust Mr. Gouin than anybody else.

The Potawatomies who, as I have said, were in league with the Ottawas for the destruction of the English but as yet had not made any great movement about the Fort, in response to Pontiac's orders kept themselves at a distance in the woods and upon the shore of the lake and river in order to stop any of the English who should be marching to the relief of the Fort. They made prisoners of two men whom the commandant at St. Joseph had dispatched from his fort with letters for Mr. Gladwin; they were caught and brought to the camp of Pontiac, who had them killed by his men.

Toward eight o'clock in the evening Pontiac sent messengers to the bad Huron band and to the Potawatomies to inform them of what had just taken place in his camp,—namely, the capture which he had made in retaining the two officers, and the secret word that the next morning at daylight he would go with four of his chiefs and traverse the region below the Fort to give new orders and to get some ammunition. He sent word to Ninivois, chief of the Potawatomies, that he was to place some twenty of his men in ambush near the Fort so that no Englishman could come out without being captured.

May 11. Wednesday.

Pontiac, like a good general, ordered thirty young men of his band to go and form an ambuscade in the vicinity of the Fort and catch all the English that came out, and from time to time to fire at the little sloop; in the meantime he and the other chiefs would go along the other shore and issue orders for the attack upon the Fort.

His men did as they were told and took up their position on the outskirts situated northeast of the Fort about one hundred and fifty yards distant. This made a good entrenchment for them. During this time Pontiac, followed by four chiefs, Mackatepelecite, Breton, Chavinon, and his nephew, went around through the woods behind the Fort and passed down into the section southwest of the Fort, and a little below. They visited all the French settlers, but chiefly those who were engaged in trade, and commanded them in a harangue to give them powder and balls, saying that if they did not wish to supply them they would plunder them of goods and all, urging as a sufficient reason that they did not need any longer to fear the English who were not in a condition to harm them any; they also declared that all the nations where there were any English in business or in garrison were making a concerted attack upon them; the Chippewas of Saginaw and those of Grand River[36] were coming to join them, and all together they would bar the entrances so that no more English could come to live in their country.

The traders, seeing themselves forced by fine words and threats, were compelled to give the Indians what they demanded in order to have peace; and by giving up part of their powder and balls they saved their property, their houses, and their families. The Potawatomies, who were at the meeting-place in obedience to Pontiac's orders, shared in the distribution, and then each left to return to his camp and distribute to their warriors and make arrangements for the attack of the following day. All this day the people

[36]Grand River was the present-day Thames of southern Ontario, which empties into Lake St. Clair after draining much of the peninsula enclosed between Lake Huron and Lake Erie. Its present name was given it by John G. Simcoe, the first Governor of the province of Upper Canada. In the French period it was commonly called La Tranche, or the Trench. The Chippewa town of Chief Sekahoe, who presently led 170 warriors to join in the siege of Detroit, was on the Grand, or Thames River.

in the Fort were quite undisturbed, the Indians not molesting them; this led a good many who were domiciled in the Fort to ask permission of the Commander to leave, and it was granted them. They withdrew with their families to the settlers along the shores, abandoning their houses and a part of their goods in the hopes that the tragic events would not last more than a few days.

Pontiac crossed the river in the afternoon with four chiefs, and went to hold a council with the Hurons in order to induce the good band to combine with them, saying that if they did not they would be attacked. The latter had not stirred from their cabins up to the present and looked with disfavor upon what was happening. Still, seeing themselves threatened and crowded so closely, and in view of the fact that they were weak, they were compelled to agree to do what the rest demanded, and promised that after mass the next day they would join the Potawatomies in the attack; they could not do so sooner because the approaching festival was too important, and without having heard mass it would be nothing but foolhardiness. Pontiac consented to delay that long, and ordered that the firing should be held back to wait for the Hurons.

May 12. Thursday; Feast of the Ascension of our Lord.

Pontiac, who knew neither feast nor Sunday and regarded all days as alike, not making profession of any religion, early in the morning ordered all his men to hold themselves ready so that as soon as the Hurons came they could attack all together. For fear that the Hurons would not keep their word he sent one of his chiefs with several young men to their camp to tell them not to fail, and as soon as their missionaries had finished the service to come and join the Potawatomies, as he only awaited their arrival to attack. The Hurons promised and kept their word.

Although Pontiac was waiting for the Hurons in order to begin the attack upon the Fort, still he had some of his men advance in order to take possession of the barns and stables around the Fort from the rear, so as to be ready to make an onslaught at the first signal and hinder anybody's leaving.

Teata and Baby, both chiefs of the good Hurons, who had preserved neutrality up to the present time and would have liked to do so longer, seeing themselves coerced by threats, ordered their band, about sixty men in number, to assemble, and they thus addressed them:

"My brothers, you see as well as we do the risks that we are running, and that in the present state of affairs we have nothing else to do but to side either with our brothers, the Ottawas and the Potawatomies, or else abandon our lands and flee with our wives and children—a rash thing to do. We would hardly get started to leave before the Ottawas and the Potawatomies, and even those of our own nation, would fall upon us and kill our wives and children and then compel us to assist them. Instead of that, by co-operating now, we make sure that our families will be left in peace in our village. We do not know what the designs of the Master of Life towards us may be. Is it He who inspires our brothers, the Ottawas, to war? If it is not He who commands it He will well be able to make his desires known, and we shall yet be able to withdraw without being stained by the blood of the English. Let us do what our brothers demand of us, and spare not."

Immediately after this harangue each chief took a tomahawk and chanted the war-song, and asked his men to do likewise while waiting for the hour of mass; after which their wives sang the mass and they listened with great devotion. When mass was over each one went to his cabin and armed himself with the necessary weapons for the attack, and then they crossed the river in twelve canoes straight to the Potawatomies who uttered yells of joy at seeing them arrive.[37] These cries were a signal to Pontiac of the arrival of the Hurons whose fire was more effective than that of all the other Indians put together.

Ninivois at the head of the Potawatomies, and Takay and Teata at the head of the Hurons, although without orders, proceeded to invest the Fort on one side, while Pontiac at the head of his men, following the same tactics, invested it on the other side; all acting together they began the attack upon the Fort and the vessels and pushed it vigorously with a heavy fire and without interruption till seven o'clock. All the time the Indians stayed in the shelter of the buildings to escape the fire from the Fort which was not able to harm them, inasmuch as there was but one cannon in fighting condition and it was only poorly supported by the musketry of the garrison. None of the shots did much damage outside the Fort, a fact which the English discovered in time. In order to remedy this and provide a better range for their guns, they tied up with iron wire several spikes in a bundle which they heated red-hot; and loading the cannon on the battery with this they fired it at two barns filled and covered with straw. In

[37]The Huron town on the Canadian shore below the Ambassador Bridge was approximately opposite the Potawatomi village in the vicinity of Twenty-third Street.

less than half an hour they were reduced to ashes. For this reason the Indians withdrew to the shelter of the other side of the hill in order to keep up the firing without risk.

During all this time the two sloops did not spare pains or powder, firing suddenly over the Fort as well as across the two ends of it, opposite which they were moored. Two Indians were killed in this action and two wounded,— one having his thigh broken and the other his arm, both by the same shot discharged toward the rear of the Fort. In this regard the English took care to conceal their killed so that the facts might not come to the knowledge of the Indians. Still it was learned in spite of them that they had several killed in the large sloop, and a good many wounded on the vessels as well as in the Fort. This was noticed by everybody who was on the inside.[38]

Toward seven o'clock in the evening the fire of the Indians having subsided a little, the Commandant, who feared that the Indians under cover of night would attempt either to carry the Fort by assault or set it on fire, issued two orders: first that tubs and barrels should be

[38]Apparently the Author's statements concerning the losses sustained by the English are erroneous. Lieutenant Jehu Hay states that but one man was wounded in the fort and another on one of the vessels. Franklin B. Hough, *Diary of the Siege of Detroit* (Albany, 1860),6.

placed in the streets and upon the ramparts at the four corners of the fort, and that the French to the number of twenty, chosen from those who were voluntarily in the Fort, should fill them by drawing water from the wells; second, in view of the fewness of numbers, which rendered defense hopeless, and since to all appearances the expected assistance would not arrive on time, and as there was a lack of supplies of food and ammunition, the French should retire to their houses and put out their fires at tattoo, and then the troops should go from the Fort to the sloops to load the goods of the officers, of themselves, and of the traders; and everybody should hold himself in readiness to embark at the first signal in order to fall back upon Niagara.

The night passed very quietly which was an augury for the English that they might hold the place longer than they had hoped, and they regained courage a little to withstand the attack of the Indians.

May 13, Friday.

It is almost a general rule that all the Indians who inhabit these regions are as unstable as the wind, and if they knew they would lose men in making war they would not begin, which sometimes induces them to stop operations as soon as they have begun; frequently, however, this arouses them the more. These, here, as I have said, had some killed and wounded; this induced them to try incantations to see how they might proceed without losing any more and take the fort which, to hear them talk, must surrender sooner or later in spite of the reinforcements which it was claimed were soon to arrive.

The Indians in the action of the preceding day had moved about so much that they were tired by night; during the evening they sought rest and slept all night and almost the following forenoon. The Commandant, who expected an attack at daybreak, had spent the whole night watching with his officers on the ramparts, ready to give orders and afraid of being surprised. When he saw how quiet the Indians were he ordered that their fortifications should be burned down at once. To this end Mr. Hopkins,[39] captain of a new company and a good soldier, made

[39]Captain Joseph Hopkins was a veteran soldier who first came to Detroit in 1762 as captain of a company he had raised, known as Hopkins' Independent Company of Rangers. He bore a prominent part in the defense of Detroit throughout the siege of 1763. Subsequently his company was disbanded and in 1764 Hopkins went to England, where he was granted a coat of arms but was otherwise disappointed in his expectation of preferment. Changing his allegiance to France, in 1766, now in San Domingo, he sought to influence Major Robert Rogers, Commandant at Mackinac, to follow his example. Denied the opportunity to serve the American colonies in the Revolution, he was living in France as late as 1794.

a sortie at the head of forty volunteers armed to the teeth, and proceeded to set fire to the suburbs which, with the exception of two houses the fire could not reach, soon burned. He then immediately returned to the Fort to allow time for another officer to make a similar expedition in another direction. This was undertaken by Mr. Hay[40], a lieutenant of the American troops, who likewise sallied out with thirty men and set fire to two barns and stables behind the Fort, and then returned at once; they suspected that

[40]Jehu Hay was a native of Chester, Pennsylvania, who in 1758 enlisted in the Sixtieth (Royal American) Regiment. In 1762 he was at Detroit with the rank of lieutenant, where he served valiantly throughout the siege of 1763. In 1776 he became deputy Indian Agent and major of Detroit militia. He served on Lieutenant Governor Hamilton's expedition to Vincennes in 1778–79 where, taken captive by George Rogers Clark, he was sent as a prisoner to Williamsburg, Va. In October, 1780 he was paroled, and a year later was exchanged. In 1782 he was appointed lieutenant-governor of Detroit, but not until July, 1784 did he assume the duties of this office. He died August 2, 1785, and was buried with much ceremony in the Governor's garden. In the summer of 1911 a coffin was uncovered by workmen engaged in digging a sewer on Jefferson Avenue, which Mr. C. M. Burton, upon investigation, was convinced contained the remains of Governor Hay. In 1764 he had married Marie Julie Réaume of Detroit. Data adapted from biographical sketch in *Burton Hist. Coll. Leaflet*, VIII, 1–16 (September, 1929). Hay kept an extensive and valuable diary of the siege of Detroit which was published by Franklin B. Hough (Ed.) at Albany in 1860, titled *Diary of the Siege of Detroit*.

Pontiac and his Indians, seeing the fires from a distance, would come and fall upon them to cut off their retreat. Fortunately, however, the Indians had something else to occupy them the whole morning. Still there were some who were on the watch, but in such few numbers that they did not dare either to show themselves or to shoot for fear of being discovered and attacked. Thus the two parties feared each other.

While these two gentlemen with part of the troops were working to render the region surrounding the fort clear and open, the Indians in Pontiac's camp were holding a council to which the oldest French settlers of the coasts had been summoned in the hope that they might be persuaded with fine words to join with them and show them how to throw up an entrenchment. The French were of no mind to do this, and anyway the most of them did not know how, and those who did know took good care not to say so, urging in their own defense that they did not know how to go about it.

Pontiac, seeing that he could not gain anything in this direction and not being willing to get by force what he had hoped to get from them voluntarily,—I mean their labor—tried another scheme and had Mr. La Butte tell Mr. Campbell to write to the Commandant what he was going to dictate to him in the presence of

all these brothers of his, the French. Mr. Campbell
did this, not wishing at all to displease a man
whose wickedness he was beginning to realize.
This letter said that Pontiac permitted the Commandant to retire with his vessels and all his
force, taking away only the clothing they wore,
just as Mr. Bellestre had done; the rest of their
goods and the goods and merchandise of the
traders should remain at the disposal of the
Indians; furthermore, it was already a good deal
that he gave them their life and he promised
that no harm should happen to them from his
followers, and he guaranteed the peace of all
the other nations. But if the Commandant was
not willing to consent to what he advised him
in that letter, he would begin the attack again
and proceed to an assault, and if he captured him
alive he would treat him as the Indians treat
one another when making war; and he was to
send a reply to him at the earliest possible moment, and do it by some Frenchman.

This letter was carried by a Frenchman to the
Commandant, who read it. Without being much
disturbed over the words of an Indian he replied
that neither he nor his officers were willing to
spite themselves in order to afford them amusement, inasmuch as by going away he ran a risk
of losing his life in his own country; and since
the King had sent him to command the Fort

he would stay there till he died, and his threats or those of other Indians did not disturb him any.

Pontiac, who had flattered himself that the Commandant would be frightened by the letter which he had written to him, and had hoped to have a chance to pillage all the merchandise of the traders, was very much taken aback to get such a dry reply from the Commandant, and at the same time to learn of the sorties which the Commandant had made to set fire to his fortifications. This was enough to make him burst with chagrin, and he ordered all his men to return to the Fort and renew the attack. They did this just as bravely as the day before, but did not come so near, having now only two buildings to hide behind and they could not all find cover. Some who were farther away fired from behind the hill and their shots passed very frequently over the Fort, yet the force of their fire disconcerted the English who were on nettles all the time for fear of an assault and undecided whether to remain or embark. The thing that reassured them was when a Frenchman who had lived a long time with the Erie Indians and had sometimes been on the warpath with them, told them about the tactics of the Indians, and declared upon his life that the Indians would never make an assault. These assurances, coming from the mouth of a disinterested man who actually knew the habits of the Indians and their behavior in war, which he described in detail to the Commandant and his officers, set their minds at rest. The firing of the Indians did not last longer than seven o'clock in the evening, except for occasional shots discharged at long range. Nevertheless the Commandant and all his officers spent this night as they did the night before, so as not to be surprised.

The Hurons did not know what took place in the camp, not having been invited to the council, and because they had received no notice they thought Pontiac would not attack and so did not come to harass the Fort at all. But having found out that some traders were coming with barges loaded with merchandise, as much for them as for the traders of the Fort, and with supplies for the English officers, they went to lie in wait for them down the river. The traders, who had no warning of what was going to befall them, when they saw the Indians upon the shore calling to them thought it was to barter deer-skins, as they do sometimes, and turned in. The Indians took them and tied them with belts; all the Frenchmen in the barges were sent away unharmed, but they took the barges with the traders and the English employees to their villages, where they killed part of them and adopted the rest. One by the name of Jacquesmane,[41] who acted as captain of the barges, was presented by the Hurons to the Potawatomies, who adopted him to live with them always. The merchandise fell into the power of the Hurons, who were so occupied with it that they forgot the Fort. There was some liquor among the supplies, and the Huron women, who feared that it would cause their husbands to do more foolish things than they had already done, threw themselves upon the barrels, knocked in their heads, and poured out all the contents, with the exception of a

[41]This was Chapman Abraham, notable as Detroit's first Jewish resident, for whom see Irving I. Katz, *The Beth El Story with a History of the Jews in Michigan before 1850* (Detroit, 1955), 22–34. Until 1783 he was engaged in trade at Detroit and elsewhere. His will, made at Montreal March 10, 1783, indicates that he died prior to April of the same year. Concerning his capture in 1763, Missionary John Heckewelder relates that his captors set about to burn him at the stake. Tied to it, and suffering from the heat of the fire that had been kindled, he begged for a drink. His torturers complied by handing him a bowl of hot liquor, which he hastily began to drink. Angered by the scalding liquid, he dashed the remaining contents of the bowl in the face of the warrior who had handed it to him. The bystanders assembled to witness the torture thereupon concluded that he was insane and at once loosed his cords and set him at liberty. Heckewelder affirms that the story he related was well known to the residents of Detroit, and was afterwards confirmed to him by Abraham himself. See Heckewelder's *Customs of the Indian Nations . . .* in *Memoirs of the Hist. Soc. of Pennsylvania*, XII, 257–58.

cask of eight gallons which an Indian rescued from the hands of a woman and hid in the woods. He divided it between them (the Hurons) and the Potawatomies, only a few of whom drank of it for fear that there might be some poison mixed in it, because somebody had given them to understand that the English wished to poison them.

May 14. Saturday.

The Indians, who had tired themselves out to no purpose the night before in firing upon the Fort, rested, waiting to begin hostilities till about ten o'clock in the morning. The Commandant gave orders to profit by this tranquillity and complete the work which had been begun the day before. This was done. A sergeant sallied out at the head of twenty volunteers from the troops and set fire to two barns which had escaped the preceding night through fear of the Indians.

When the sortie was accomplished the incendiaries returned and the space around the Fort was free. One could easily observe all that happened from the stockade of the Fort to the very top of the hill which was a keen disappointment to the Indians, who, as soon as they saw this expedition, ran to hinder it, thinking to arrive soon enough, but they were greatly surprised when they found nothing which could protect them from the fire of the Fort except the other side of the hill, behind which they stationed themselves in order to commence the same operations as in the two preceding days.

The English, who were expecting this, were not surprised to hear the battle begin again. They began to get used to these tactics, yet feared an assault in view of the warning a Frenchman from without gave them in the night that the Indians would try an onslaught; and the behavior of the Indians on this day more than the other two rendered them almost sure that such was their plan.

In this extremity the English had no other resource but to betake themselves to their vessels, where their goods had been moved the first day, and set sail for Niagara. However, this was not done because they were told that if they could pass this third day, which was drawing to a close, without an assault, the Indians would never try it, for they knew well they would lose a number of men by storming,— a thing they greatly feared. The day passed like the preceding ones; the officers stood guard with their troops day and night, wearing themselves out and causing their men almost to drop with fatigue.

Father Potier, Jesuit missionary to the Hurons, by virtue of his calling and the power that he had over them had kept a part of them, especially the good band, within the bounds of neutrality by refusing them the sacrament. In order to succeed in restraining them all, he needed help, and asked Mr. Laboise[42], a resident of the Fort but who for some time had been living at his house, to be kind enough to cross the river and invite for him the oldest and most sensible of the settlers whom he knew the Indians loved and esteemed to come and join him in trying to arrest the course of that storm, which in threatening the English, seemed also to threaten the French. This was done. These settlers who knew and respected the Jesuit father for a worthy priest and regarded him as a saint upon earth, hastened at this call to assemble at his place and deliberate over what should be done to mollify Pontiac, and what representation should be made to get him to end this internal war.

After counseling together the most respected among the French, twelve in number, went to the camp of Pontiac, who was greatly surprised

[42]A footnote at this point in the C. M. Burton edition of the Journal states that a Joseph Poupard *dit* Laboise was living in Detroit at this time. A note in Mr. Burton's hand in the Poupard genealogy in Denissen, Detroit Genealogies (Ms.) states that Poupard was the interpreter who accompanied Major Robert Rogers' expedition to Detroit in 1760. However, the Poupard family alternative surname was Lafleur instead of Laboise. It seems probable to the present Editor that the name "Laboise," herein noted, was a variant spelling for Labrose (Labrosse), who is noted *post*, 103, as Dominic Jourdain *dit* Labrosse.

to see them and asked the occasion of their visit. Seeing he was of such an affable manner they flattered themselves upon their sure success, and told him they had come on a good errand. At this Pontiac asked them to enter the house of Mr. Baptiste Meloche where Messrs. Campbell and McDougall, his two prisoners, were; he summoned his chiefs to come and hear the good words of their brothers, the Frenchmen. When everyone had arrived the oldest French resident spoke in the name of all the settlers and asked Pontiac what his intentions were in regard to the war. The latter replied that he had no other design than to expel the English from the Fort and from their lands in order to make a place for the French commander, who, as he had heard, was about to arrive. The French represented to him that if he expected a French commander so soon he had only to remain quiet in his lodge, for there would be time enough to strike after he had arrived. He replied that he had promised to have the place ready for his Father, and that he wished him to find it so.

The Frenchmen protested in vain that the war would ruin them and prevent them from going about their business affairs, and they made use of the most telling Indian terms to express to him their trouble. Pontiac, who persisted in the same views and was moved by nothing, answered that in order to be the sooner relieved all they had to do was to join with him in driving out the English, after which they could retire to their lands and wait for the French who were sure to come. The settlers replied that it was impossible for them to do this, because they had promised to be loyal to the English.

And so, not being able to gain anything on either side, the French were constrained to return and report to Father Potier, who gave them an exhortation on the subject of the present calamities and begged them to pray with fervor to bend the will of Heaven, which was chastening them through this war. They promised to do this and all returned to their homes more fatigued from their useless trip than satisfied with the success of their enterprise.

May 15. Sunday.

The Indians, who had spent the three preceding days doing nothing, resolved to keep quiet till the arrival of reinforcements which were expected from the Chippewas of Grand River, and it was reported they would not be long in coming; they thought with this addition to their numbers they would the more easily succeed in their foolish plans.

The English, who had spent a very peaceful night and not detected any movement on the part of the Indians, thought that things were not as bad as they had appeared at the beginning. The Commandant, who had never lost courage, although somewhat uneasy, ordered the garden of Mr. La Butte to be destroyed during this respite. This was done by Mr. Hay, an officer, who sallied out at the head of forty volunteers and proceeded to spoil the garden. The fence was of cedar stakes ten feet tall and enclosed a quantity of fruit trees and a house where the gardener lived, a very great advantage to the Indians. They pulled up the stakes, burnt the house, cut down the trees, and threw them into the river. It did not take them long to do this and they returned as peacefully as they went out.

One must not think the Indians did not see them doing this, but they perceived that it was too late to hinder their shelter's being destroyed and so kept quiet until one o'clock in the afternoon when they fired a shot at the little sloop. But it was just so much time and powder wasted for them.

The English officers, who up to the present had hardly had time to breathe, seeing that it looked as if they would not be disturbed during the day, caused half of the troops to rest till evening; the others worked to make the two cannon of some value which had not been used up to this time because of lack of a place to mount them. The Commandant ordered that embrasures should be made on both sides of the big gate of the Fort which faced the high road toward the southwest to receive these two pieces, one of which commanded the high road, and the other the fields and the house of Mr. Jacques St. Martin[43] in the same direction.

May 16. Monday.

The Commandant, who had learned that the good band of the Hurons had withdrawn from the plot through the efforts of Father Potier, their missionary, and had gone to another locality

[43]Jean Baudry lived in the parish of St. Martin des Buttes (St. Martin on the Heights) in Luché, province of Anjou, France. His son, Urban, born in 1621, migrated to Canada, where he settled at Three Rivers and was buried under the church Aug. 23, 1682. From the parental birthplace in Anjou were derived the subsequent family surnames of St. Martin and Des Buttes, to create confusion for future historians.

A grandson of Urban Baudry, Jean Baptiste Baudry *dit* Des Buttes *dit* St. Martin, was born at Three Rivers, July 3, 1684. He married at Quebec, Oct. 8, 1721, Marie Louise Doyon, a relative of Madam Marie Therese Cadillac, wife of the founder of Detroit. The couple lived for many years in Quebec, where all of their children were born.

They subsequently removed to Detroit, where Jean Baptiste became interpreter to the Hurons. On April 1, 1750 he obtained a grant of land immediately west of the fort which is now the easterly portion of the Cass farm or Private Claim No. 55. Here he died and on Nov. 20, 1755 was buried "under the second pew on the Epistle's side of the church." The house which he occupied (demol-

so as not to be concerned in it any more, resolved to give the bad band reason to repent of
their foolishness by sending the big sloop to
cannonade and set on fire their villages if it was
possible, and to do the same to the Potawatomies
while on the way.

The expedition was put in charge of Captain
Hopkins who with Mr. Hay, an officer, and ten
soldiers and a trader embarked in the big sloop.
The wind having turned into the east seemed
to wish to favor them in this enterprise. They

ished in 1882) was the storied Cass mansion, the most
notable residence in the City's history. According to legend it may have been built by Cadillac in 1703 as a present
for the friendly Huron chief, Quarante Sols; more probably, perhaps, it was built by Baudry at some date prior
to 1750. Baudry had two sons, Joseph Mary Baudry *dit*
Des Buttes *dit* St. Martin, born at Quebec in 1725, and
Jacques Baudry *dit* Des Buttes *dit* St. Martin, born there
in 1733, who succeeded their father as interpreters to the
Hurons. Jacques, who commonly went by the name of St.
Martin, married Marie Anne Navarre on Oct. 28, 1760,
daughter of Robert Navarre, the royal notary in the
French period. He continued to live in the parental home
until his death in June, 1768. Harassed on either side, by
the Indians using his house as a shelter and by the English who trained their guns upon it, on July 1, 1763 he
sought and obtained permission from Gladwin to take
shelter with his family in the Fort. Father Christian Denissen states that Jacques Baudry was "promiscuously"
called Des Buttes and St. Martin. Data adapted from
Denissen, Detroit Genealogies (Ms.) and M. M. Quaife,
"The Mansion of St. Martin" in *Burton Hist. Coll. Leaflet,*
III, 33–48 (January, 1925).

lifted anchor to drop down to the right of the
two villages, but had not made a third of a mile
before the wind changed to the south and came
on to blow, and they had it for the once almost
ahead. It was necessary to tack in order to run
where they wanted to go, and this they did.

This maneuver frightened the French settlers,
who for the most part did not understand it, for
they believed that the English had a grudge
against them and that the vessel was dropping
down the river only to lay waste their coasts
and set fire to their houses. This last they could
not have done, not having any forge on board.
Nevertheless, there were some who went to hide
their goods in ditches in their fields, and others
who concealed theirs in the woods. Other Frenchmen who understood the movements of the boat
came and reassured them, showing them the
unreasonableness of their fears; but the thing
that reassured them more was an accident which
happened to the boat and which would have
caused its absolute destruction if there had been
any Indians around. The wind which kept getting stronger was no longer favorable to the
vessel, still the English, who were absolutely
bent on reaching the two villages, held up to the
wind, tacking from one shore to the other. As
they were coming about in order to stand out
again, there came a puff of wind which filled

the sails and stranded the sloop about twenty feet from shore and five-eighths of a mile from the Fort. There they were almost on shore a quarter of an hour, and at great risk they had to carry out an anchor two hundred feet into the river in order to work themselves afloat. They finally succeeded, and returned to the anchorage they had started from, very well pleased at having escaped the clutches of the Indians, for it is certain that ten Indians could have captured the boat in the situation in which it was, in spite of any defense they could have made, and their imprudence would have cost them dear.

There were Indians enough, indeed, who beheld the vessel from a distance and came to attack it, but when they arrived it was too late; and they could console themselves with this proverb: "The wolf escapes when the dog stops to ——." However, the rage they felt at having missed a chance so favorable led them to come and open fire on the Fort from about two P. M. till six, but without killing as much as a fly. The French who had remained in the Fort drew water from the wells and filled the vessels placed to receive it.

May 17. Tuesday.

Pontiac, who had not taken care in the beginning of the war to lay in any provisions for the sustenance of his warriors, was obliged to resort to fraud in order to live,—he and all his followers. To this end he and four chiefs of his nation visited all the settlers of the coasts to levy contributions of food, saying they could give voluntarily or under compulsion,—if not they would have their live stock killed, a thing which was already begun. In spite of the fact that there were settlers who were already feeding as many as twenty Indians, this did not keep them from committing depredations.

The settlers, who feared that the Indians would combine against them, agreed to the demand of the chiefs, and each one supported the savages who lived in his vicinity. Pontiac and his people derived their supplies from the North Coast, Ninivois and the Potawatomies from the Southwest, and the Hurons from the East and South.

About ten o'clock, when each nation had looked after the food supplies, the chiefs of all the nations met at Pontiac's camp and deliberated as to how the Frenchmen outside the Fort might be kept from entering, and those inside from coming out; they did this because they said those from within carried to the outside information of what happened inside, and those on the outside carried to the Fort what passed without, and all this did not result in any good. Their reasoning was not bad, because actually there were some

French who sowed dissension under the pretext of wishing to restore harmony between the two parties. It was therefore concluded in the council that there should be a guard of twenty men from the two nations at each side of the Fort who should guard the approaches of the two sides in order to hinder the going and coming of people, and that those who tried to pass in spite of them should be fired upon. What was agreed upon was done. Some Frenchmen who wanted to try to pass came within one of getting shot. In the course of the afternoon there was some firing on both sides, but no harm done.

May 18. Wednesday.

The Indians, who were occupied with a plan they had pondered on for some time, namely, to send a message to Mr. De Neyon[44] among the Illinois, neglected the Fort for the whole day. Pontiac had all the chiefs and leading men of

[44]The Chevalier Pierre Joseph Neyon de Villiers, Commandant since 1755 of Fort de Chartres. During his incumbency he endeavored to restrain the Indian tribes from making war upon the English. On June 15, 1764 he left the Illinois for New Orleans with most of his troops and many of the civilian inhabitants. He later returned to France, where he became a brigadier general in 1775 and died in 1779. On December 1, 1763 he wrote to his superior expressing his confidence that he could have prevented the Indian war altogether if only General Amherst had given him timely notice of the conclusion of peace between France and England. See *Illinois Hist. Colls.*, X, 50.

each nation assemble for a council, and he sent messengers to all the oldest of the French settlers and to those he knew to invite them to the council, to which the two officers who were prisoners among them were admitted. When everybody had come Pontiac took a war-belt, and addressing all said:

"My brothers, you are ignorant of the reasons which have induced me to act, although I have spared no pains to keep you informed of my sentiments. But as I fear that our Father will not come and take possession of the Fort soon enough after I have expelled or killed the English, and that the Indians may insult you if there is no commandant here to obviate this difficulty, I have resolved to send to the Illinois some of our French brothers with some Indians to carry our war-belts and our words to our Father, Mr. De Neyon, and ask him to send us a French officer for a commandant to guide us and replace the English. You, my brothers, will do me a pleasure to write to our Father in this matter, joining your words to mine."

He at once had a letter written to Mr. De Neyon in the presence of these two English officers, telling about the council and all the reasons which had induced him to act, just as I have described in the beginning of this narrative. To this was added a letter from the French, who earnestly begged Mr. De Neyon, in view of the present circumstances, to restrain the tribes.[45]

When these letters were finished Pontiac, who presided over everything, named the two Frenchmen and the two Indians whom he wanted to carry the letters and his words, at the same time telling them that they should hold themselves in readiness to depart the next morning, and that those who wanted to go along, either French or Indian, might announce themselves and he would not prevent them, and he would have the settlers give them all that they would need for the expedition.[46]

May 19. Thursday.

Pontiac, who believed that Mr. De Neyon would be able to furnish a commandant in reply

---

[45]For these letters see Peckham, *Pontiac and the Indian Uprising,* 147–49; *Mich. Pioneer Colls.,* XXVII, 644–45.

[46]The Frenchmen who elected to accompany the mission were Jacques Godfroy, Mini Chêne, a Beaubien, a Chauvin, and a Labadie. Apparently Godfroy and Chêne were designated by Pontiac and the others were volunteers. For Godfroy see *ante,* 49. "Mini" Chêne was Leopold, son of Charles Chêne and Catherine Sauvage and a nephew of the interpreter, Pierre Chêne *dit* La Butte. Leopold was himself an official interpreter. He had children by an Ottawa woman and by a Sauteuse. By the latter he had a son, Charles, who was baptized Oct. 25, 1775. He lived on a farm east of the Fort which was granted to him by Pontiac, Sept. 17, 1765. He died January 13, 1778. Data adapted from footnote in C. M. Burton edition of the *Journal,* 111.

to his demand, had nothing else to do the next morning but supply the needs of those whom he was sending away. He helped them embark and told them to go and wait for him below the fort at the mill, and he would make the rounds of the region to get them provisions. This he did, going from house to house demanding of each one, according to his ability, food and ammunition for the messengers so as to enable them to depart promptly. When all the outfit for the trip was delivered to the men, they set out for the Illinois about ten o'clock.

As soon as the messengers had gone Pontiac returned to his camp and commanded his young men to go and amuse themselves by harassing the vessels, because he knew well enough that they could not do them any great harm. They did this till toward five o'clock, when they got tired of shooting and returned to the camp in order to rest from their useless labor.

May 20. Friday.

The Commandant, who had a plan to send one of the sloops to Niagara to hasten the arrival of reinforcements which he had been expecting for a long time, gave orders to Mr. Le Grand[47], ap-

[47]Gabriel Christopher Legrand was a native of France of noble parentage who enlisted in the army and came to Detroit as surgeon major of the garrison. On April 17, 1758 he married Marie Madeline Chapoton, who died January 7, 1763 (for her will see *Burton Hist. Coll. Leaflet,* III, 9–

pointed judge in place of Mr. St. Cosme[48], that all the French in the Fort should pick up the stones which they might find in the streets and carry them to the edge of the river to ballast the vessel which was about to sail. The boats changed places and the soldiers put the stones on board the little sloop.

The day passed without any hostility on either side.

May 21. Saturday.

At eleven o'clock in the morning the little sloop sailed from in front of the Fort for the

10 (September, 1924). Legrand married (second) Veronica Réaume on July 26, 1764. He was a man of some local influence, serving both as notary and as judge. Of his work as notary C. M. Burton observes: "He seems to have been incompetent for some reason, and not finding sufficient employment in Detroit he wandered off to Kaskaskia to reside, and there succeeded in getting the land titles so badly mixed up that the land commissioners made loud complaint of his inefficiency." *City of Detroit, Michigan, 1703–1922*, I, 169; Fannie Anderson, *Doctors Under Three Flags*, 18–19.

[48]Pierre Laurence St. Cosme was a native of Lower Canada who came to Detroit prior to January 25, 1747, on which date he married here Catherine Lootman *dit* Barrois. He was a magistrate, as here noted, prior to 1763. In 1768 he was one of four residents delegated by the townsmen as their representatives in rebuilding the stockade around the town. This same year he served as one member of a committee of ten appointed by the Commandant to investigate the official conduct of Justice Philip Dejean. He was buried Sept. 21, 1787. See *The John Askin Papers*. I, 212.

entrance to Lake Erie in order to discover if the expected reinforcements were coming. She was ordered to stay there a week, reconnoitering, in order to expedite the arrival of reinforcements, and at the end of that time to go on to Niagara.

The Indians, either from laziness or from contempt, did not approach to fire on the Fort or the vessel at all during the whole day. About five o'clock in the evening it was learned through a Frenchman who had sallied out that Sekahos, great chief of the Chippewas of Grand River, had arrived in response to Pontiac's demand with one hundred twenty men of his band.

May 22. Sunday; Whitsunday.

During the whole of this sacred day there was a violent wind and a downpour of rain which caused both sides to remain quiet.

May 23. Monday.

The weather of the morning, which had not cleared up from the day before, kept the Indians quiet. The Commandant, who was suspicious of them and foresaw that the tranquility would not last long, having been warned, besides, to be on his guard against any surprise, ordered that the iron and steel in the warehouse should be used to make tomahawks, daggers, spears, and hooks with which to arm his soldiers against an assault, in case the Indians should want to attempt one. Two French blacksmiths in the Fort did this work.

About four P. M. a rumor reached the Fort and got to the officers that the Indians intended to set fire to the Fort and the stockade, and the houses within, by means of fire arrows. However, they could not possibly do this, fortunately not having any of the necessary materials. But from prudence and fear of surprise ladders were placed upon the royal magazine and the houses, and on the ground by them tubs full of water to serve in case of need. The Commandant ordered that not a Frenchman in the Fort should go to bed, but make a night of it, and that they should assemble three or four together in their houses in order to be ready at the first call.

About two o'clock in the afternoon the weather cleared up, and it was expected the Indians would make some attack with the return of fair weather, but they did not, and the remainder of the day passed as had the morning.

May 24. Tuesday.

The Indians, who had been idle all the day before, continued so on this day up to four o'clock, when they shook off the yoke of laziness to recommence their hostility against the Fort, and they did not cease till midnight. They were no more satisfied then than if they had kept quiet, unless it was that they had used up powder and ball to no purpose.

The Commandant, who foresaw that this tragic

affair would not end soon, and that it would not be easy to get provisions from without, from fear of being in need before the return of the vessel and the arrival of the convoy, which was expected any day, in order to avoid this, commanded that all the houses of the French should be visited and whatever superfluous food each man might have should be taken and stored for the sustenance of all his forces. This order was carried out by Officer Hay, the Commissary, and the Judge[49], who went into all the houses and collected wheat, flour, peas, also the corn belonging to the

[49]The Judge was Gabriel Legrand. The Commissary was Sampson Fleming, who was appointed Deputy Commissary at Detroit on Feb. 5, 1762. He remained in this office until September, 1779, when, dissatisfied with a reduction in rank and pay by Nathaniel Day, Commissary General at New York, he tendered his resignation, asking that it be accepted "immediately." On June 17, 1768 he married at Detroit Alice Haliburton, daughter of Rev. William Haliburton, who according to more or less accurate family tradition came from Ireland to Canada about the year 1757 to serve as chaplain in the Sixtieth, or Royal American Regiment. Through the subsequent remarriages of his widow, Alice became the stepdaughter of William Forsyth, noted Detroit innkeeper, and the half-sister of John Kinzie of early Chicago fame. Fleming removed from Detroit to New York City, where, following his death, his widow married Nicholas Low. Their descendants were prominent there and elsewhere until within recent years. Data adapted from sketch by the present Editor in Mrs. John H. Kinzie's *Wau-Bun. The "Early Day" in the Northwest* (Chicago, 1932), XXX–XXXIV; and from Fleming Mss. in Burton Hist. Collection.

Indians which the French were storing, and which the Indians had not the precaution to take away before beginning their beautiful fiasco. The officers also collected oil, tallow, and, in general, everything which could serve for food, keeping an account of everything they took, and especially the names of the persons to whom the provisions belonged, assuring these of payment, at the same time giving them receipts for the same. Only the Indian corn belonging to the savages was confiscated for the general good. All the provisions were placed in the royal warehouse to serve as a defense against the famine which threatened the English.

May 25. Wednesday.

The Indians, who had worn themselves out during a part of the preceding night wasting ammunition, rested till almost five o'clock in the afternoon before recommencing the attack, as upon the day before. Only the chiefs and old men did not take a hand in the firing, and while the others rested they strolled about to discover what was passing and guard against surprise, suspecting the English all the time.

The French settlers of the coasts were torn by conflicting feelings; some of them, who were actually honest and moved by sentiments of humanity and religion, groaned over the foolish enterprise of the Indians, and would willingly have sacrificed even the last bit of their property to check the Indian nations and bring about peace in the region; others, who were governed by a feeling of unreasonable hostility, and had never cherished any sentiments of submission or respect, would gladly have cast their lot with the Indians had it not been for the fear of public contempt; still others were in a vacillating condition, not knowing which of the two parties to join. But all alike, worn out as they were by conflicting opinions and the behavior of the Indians, had already assembled at different times at the houses of the oldest settlers to deliberate over some means of checking the Indians. The day before they had resolved that they ought to go to the camp and ask Pontiac for a council, and try to find out what his intentions were concerning the war.

To this end they selected fifteen whom the Indians knew and esteemed, who proceeded to the camp and asked for a parley. Pontiac, who had not been notified of this visit, was surprised at it, and suspected some mystery which he as yet could not fathom. Nevertheless he received them cordially and asked what had brought them; his curiosity did not permit him to wait until they had themselves stated the reason for their visit. They all replied with one accord that they had come to talk over some business, and that they would be pleased to have all his chiefs hear what they had to say. Pontiac, who was anxious to know what the matter was, sent messengers to the Potawatomies and the Hurons of the bad band, and they came in a short time. When they were all assembled the most respected member of the delegation, taking the great chief by the hand, addressed them all:

"My brothers, you seem surprised to see us. We have come here only to renew the ancient alliance which our fathers made with you, and which you are today destroying by bringing death upon us. When you began your attack upon the English you gave us to understand that you would do us no wrong. It is true you do us no personal harm, but it is nevertheless doing us harm to do what you are doing in killing our live stock. When they are all killed how do you think we shall be able to plow our fields, to sow, and make bread for you? If only in killing them you did not waste half you would profit the more and hold out the longer, and we should not lose so much.

"When you enter our homes you enter with the tomahawk raised as if you intended to kill us while begging for food. Have we ever refused at any time when you have asked us? You do not speak to us any more like brothers, but like masters, and you treat us as we treat our slaves. Since when have you seen the Indians domineering over the French? Is this the way you promised your Father Bellestre, when he departed, that you would love and cherish your French brothers? Avenge the insults which have been offered you—we do not object to this—but remember that we are all brothers and the children of your Great Father, the King of France. You are expecting him back, you say. When he returns to supply your needs, as he has already done, and sees that you have killed us and taken all that we were preserving for him, what will he say to you? Do you think he will give you presents to cover up the wrong you have done us? On the contrary, he will regard you as rebellious children and traitors, and instead of petting you he will make war upon you, and then you will have two nations upon you, the French and the English. Consider whether you want to have two enemies, or whether you will live as brothers among us."

Pontiac, who had not lost a single word of all that had been said, in the name of all the chiefs made reply to the French:

"My brothers, we have never planned to do you any injury or harm, neither have we intended that any should be done you, but among my young men there are some, as among you, who are always doing harm in spite of all precautions that one can take. Moreover, it is not for personal

vengeance merely that I am making war upon the
English; it is for you, my brothers, as well as for
us. When the English have insulted us in the
councils which we have held with them, they
have insulted you, too, without your knowing it.
And since I and all my brothers, also, know that
the English have taken away from you all means
to avenge yourselves by disarming you and making you sign a paper which they have sent to
their own country,—a thing they could not do
to us,—for this reason we wish to avenge you
equally with ourselves, and I swear the destruction of all that may be upon our lands.

"What is more, you do not know all the reasons which oblige me to act as I do. I have told
you only what concerns you, but you will know
the rest in time. I know very well that many of
you, my brothers, consider me a fool, but you will
see in the future if I am what people say I am,
and if I am wrong. I know very well, also, that
there are some among you, my brothers, who
side with the English in making war upon us and
that grieves me. As for them, I know them well
and when our Great Father returns I shall name
and point them out to him and they will see
whether they or we will be most satisfied with
the result in the end.

"I do not doubt, my brothers, that this war
causes you annoyance because of the movements

of our brothers who are coming and going in your homes constantly; I am chagrined at it, but do not think, my brothers, that I inspire the harm which is being done you. As a proof that I do not desire it just recall to mind the war with the Foxes, and the way I behaved as regards you seventeen years ago. Now when the Chippewas and Ottawas of Michilimackinac, and all the northern nations, came with the Sauk and Foxes to destroy you, who was it that defended you? Was it not I and my men?

"When Mackinac, the great chief of all these nations, said in his council that he would carry the head of your commander to his village, and devour his heart, and drink his blood, did I not take up your cause and go to his village and tell him that if he wanted to kill the French he would have to begin first with me and my men?[50] Did I not help you rid yourselves of them and drive them away? How does it come then, my brothers, that you would think me today ready to turn my weapons against you? No, my

[50]Evidently Pontiac alludes to the plot of Nicolas to destroy Detroit in 1746, for whose frustration he now claims credit. Obviously the French settlers whom he was addressing must have known the facts concerning the affair. This consideration sheds interesting light upon Pontiac's chiefly unknown earlier career. See Peckham, *Pontiac and the Indian Uprising*, 32-33; Thomas J. Maxwell, Jr., "Pontiac before 1763" in *Ethnohistory*, IV, 41-46 (Winter No., 1957).

brothers, I am the same French Pontiac who helped you seventeen years ago; I am French, and I want to die French, and I repeat that it is altogether your interests and mine that I avenge. Let me carry out my plan. I do not demand your assistance, because I know you could not give it; I only ask you for provisions for myself and all my followers. If, however, you should like to help me I would not refuse; you would please me and get out of trouble the quicker, for I promise when the English shall be driven away from here, or killed, we shall all withdraw into our villages, following our custom, to await the coming of our French Father.

"Thus you see, my brothers, what my sentiments are. Do not worry. I shall see to it that neither my followers nor any other Indians harm you any further, but I ask that our women may have permission to raise our corn upon your fields and fallow lands. By allowing this you will oblige us greatly."

All the French replied that they were very willing. The council came to an end and the Frenchmen withdrew, satisfied with their negotiations with Pontiac. The very same day the Indian women began work in the corn fields, and several settlers ploughed fields for the planting, and that same afternoon Pontiac went all along the shores to give orders concerning the subsistence of all the Indians so that nothing more might be taken from the settlers by force.

The Commandant had observed that the Potawatomies in camp southwest of the Fort since the departure of the sloop, came along the river edge under the shelter of the bank in which were two lime-kilns, and stationed themselves in ambush behind these to fire upon the soldiers who were accustomed to go down to the river for their needs. In order to keep the Indians from coming any more to annoy them from that side, he ordered a portable bastion, or cavalier, to be built and placed on the shore to defend the edge of the river so that people could go down there without danger. Two carpenters and several persons who knew how to handle the axe were set to work upon this structure in the parade-ground. And since there were no timbers in the Fort suitable for this task, the workmen took the walks from in front of the houses and used them in the construction of this building which was ready for erection at five o'clock in the evening. To place this structure in the designated spot, it became necessary to carry the timbers from the Fort piece by piece. All the French in the Fort, together with some soldiers of the garrison, were ordered out, and they all passed the timbers through a postern which had been made to mount a cannon on the river side. When once the materials were on the outside it was no easy task to mortise and bolt them together because of the weight, but the eagerness of everybody to help enabled them to get around the difficulty when they came to it. When the structure was put together they tried to raise it, but did not succeed for two reasons: firstly, not enough men; secondly, and this was the greater reason, when the Indians who were in ambush in a ditch two hundred yards away saw some English among the French and recognized that the structure was going to be an obstacle for them, they fired several times upon everybody, and this caused the work to be abandoned on the spot. The erection was put over to the next day at dawn.

May 26. Thursday.

At the peep of day the French with some soldiers were ordered to raise the bastion which they had been compelled to abandon on account of the Indians, who were now resting in their camps. This fact gave them time to mount it more easily, but they worked with all possible vigilance. As they were finishing and preparing to retire, a Frenchman thought he would stroll out towards the kilns; he was nearly shot by an Indian hidden in one of the kilns, who ran as soon as he had fired to hide himself farther away in a trench where some others were. The Frenchman, who mistrusted there were others, came back as fast as he could and re-entered the fort with the rest.

During this time a Frenchman by the name of Labrosse,[51] a resident of the Fort, who had gone out the day before with permission on a matter of business, returned with the news of the capture of Fort Sandusky by the Hurons of the bad tribe. These had actually passed the night previous along the other shore of the river with a red flag flying from the stern of one of their canoes. Several had seen this but could not discover what it meant, though they suspected that the Indians had made some new capture. This was confirmed by the report of this man, who told how he had seen the commandant of the captured place, and that the garrison had been slaughtered, the fort burned, and all the property, not only of the troops but of the traders there, plundered.[52]

[51]Dominic Jourdain *dit* Labrosse, whose father, Paul Raymond Jourdain *dit* Labrosse, was a sculptor and organ-builder of Montreal. Dominic was born there on August 12, 1730. He migrated to Detroit, where on August 18, 1755 he married Jane Cardinal. He was buried at Assumption Church, Sandwich, Nov. 19, 1816. An entry in Hugh Heward's Journal from Detroit to the Illinois in 1790 indicates that Labrosse then had a mill on the Canadian shore below Detroit. See Denissen, Detroit Genealogies (Ms.), and *The John Askin Papers,* I, 339.

[52]Fort Sandusky was taken by stratagem on May 16 and all of the fifteen-man garrison save Lieutenant Chris-

The Commandant of the Fort said he would not believe anything of this until he saw a letter from the officer, who was at the time a prisoner among the Ottawas, where the Hurons had taken him. This poor man upon his arrival had been very badly treated by the other Indians, who as they landed struck him with clubs and their fists and made him yell till he reached their camp.[53] Here he was adopted at once by an Indian woman who had lost her husband; out of pity she took him for her second husband and in this way his life was saved.

Pontiac and the Ottawas, who had learned from the Hurons upon their return that the little sloop was still at the mouth of the river, formed the plan of capturing her. To this end they went down early in the morning to the village of the Potawatomies and confided their project to them. The Potawatomies joined them in great glee, as if the affair was already accomplished. The Ottawas took with them their prisoner, Mr. Campbell, and his interpreter, Mr. La Butte, hoping that the presence of this

topher Pauli were slain. Pauli was carried to Detroit, where his reception by the triumphant savages is adequately narrated by our Author. On July 3 he eluded the attentions of his unwelcome bride by making his escape into the fort.

[53]In accordance with savage custom he was made to run the gantlet.

officer would lead the people of the vessel to surrender.[54] But in this they were greatly mistaken. The men on the sloop would not hear to it, and their only reply to the Indians was by cannon and gun shots; this compelled the savages to withdraw till evening, when they thought they would succeed better. But the crew of the vessel, who were fast getting better acquainted with their tricks, suspecting that the Indians would make some new attempt in the night to capture them, and seeing that there were only seven men of them and that with this little force they could not long repulse two hundred, resolved to run for it. And so to frustrate the hopes of the Indians and to save themselves and the vessel from their clutches, they lifted anchor in the night and sailed for the open lake, heading for Niagara in accordance with the orders they had received from the Commandant when they left the Fort.

[54]Lieutenant Hay relates that Pontiac told Campbell he was taking him along to put in one of the canoes to order the captain of the *Michigan* to surrender her to the savages. The brave Scotchman's answer was that Pontiac might put him to death but he would not go. Although Pontiac forced him to go with the Indians, according to Parkman when the crucial moment arrived he merely called out to the crew of the vessel to do their duty, regardless of the consequences to him. See Hough, *Diary of the Siege of Detroit,* 13; Francis Parkman, *Conspiracy of Pontiac* (Boston, 1913 ed.), I, 261.

May 27. Friday.

The Indians, who had tired themselves out to no purpose in their attempt to capture the sloop, luckily for the boat and those on board having failed in their project, returned to their camp with Mr. Campbell and the interpreter and remained there all day. There was no hostility on either side.

May 28. Saturday.

The Indians remained inactive all day. This was due to the fact that they were awaiting news of reinforcements which, according to a runner who had come in the night, ought to arrive during the course of the day. For this reason they did not come to annoy the Fort. However, they were false to the promises which they had made the settlers and began again to kill and steal their live stock.

Toward five o'clock in the afternoon a very large number of Indians were seen in the woods behind the Fort. They came from the direction of the lake, going toward their camp; they waved scalps and uttered twenty death-cries mingled with yells of joy to announce that they had just come from an attack upon some place. It was the rest of those who had captured Fort Sandusky. At the same time a rumor reached the Fort that all the French who had gone in the employ of the English traders to Michilimackinac had been killed by the Chippewas and Ottawas of that place. This report, which lacked confirmation, turned out later to be false.

The Commandant ordered a sortie when he saw that the Indians were quiet. This was carried out by Mr. Hay, an officer, with twenty men, for the purpose of destroying an intrenchment which the Indians had made in the night to the southwest of the Fort, one hundred and twenty-five yards distant from the gate. The Hurons and Potawatomies had come by stealth in the darkest part of the night to the fence of Mr. St. Martin, and taking some timbers almost twenty feet long which were near the fort had piled them up in two tiers to the height of a man, and had planted stakes in front and behind to support them. In this way, hidden behind these beams, they did not fear the balls from the cannon which faced them.

In the morning this work was discovered by the sentinels, who informed the Commandant at once, and it was destroyed in its very inception, as it were, by these twenty men. They burned the fence, carried the timbers to the Fort, and cleared the field in such a way that no one could approach the Fort in the night as near as sixty-five yards without being seen.

May 29. Sunday.

The weather was unsettled all day, thus affording rest to both sides.

May 30. Monday.

The English had a seine which had not been used since the beginning of this fatal trouble. Several young Frenchmen asked for it, saying they would catch them some fish while catching some for themselves. It was got ready for them, and two soldiers who knew how to handle it were sent to help them. But they did not have a chance to catch a single fish, or even to cast the net in the water; the Indians, who were in ambush in a ditch three hundred and fifty yards from the Fort, saw them without being seen. Knowing very well that the French did not make use of the seine for their own fishing, they suspected that they were only helping the English. They fired several times upon the fishermen and their boat, so that they landed quickly and returned to the fort no better off than when they went out with the seine, which was never used again.

Around nine o'clock in the forenoon a soldier strolling along the sentry-walk talking with a sentinel in the flag bastion which faces the river saw some craft appearing at Montreal Point[55] on

[55]Montreal Point (*La Pointe de Montreal*) was the western extremity of the crescent of land on the south side of the river, extending from the lower end of Belle Isle to Petit Cote, opposite the end of the West Boulevard [Grand Boulevard] in Detroit—land on which the Huron Mission was built." Footnote by C. M. Burton in 1912 edition of the Journal. The mission lands were approxi-

the Huron village side of the river. The objects appeared to be barges with people in them. This soldier, as well as all the others, knew that the convoy was expected at any time with relief of provisions and men, and he hurried to notify the officer of the guard of what he had just seen. The officer, convinced, went to inform the Commandant and the other officers. All these came with the troops and traders and climbed upon the bastion in order themselves to verify the soldier's report and find out exactly what it was. They saw with a field glass that it was really the convoy which had been so long expected. This caused great joy through the hope that the reinforcements arriving would change the attitude of the Indians. However, the joy was short-lived, being killed in its very birth, for it was interrupted by a number of war-cries which could be heard from the same place where the boats were in sight; it immediately gave place to gloom and forebodings for the convoy, because they thought then that the Indians had discovered

---

mately those occupied today by the parish of the Assumption in Sandwich. Huron Line Road, which now passes alongside the church, marks the eastern end of the former Huron village. George Paré, *The Catholic Church in Detroit,* 189–90. The guess may be hazarded that the name of the Point was bestowed by the early settlers of Detroit because boats coming from Montreal could first be seen from the town when they passed this point.

and captured the boats and killed the men. And this was the case.

The Hurons of the evil band and the Potawatomies had learned some days before that the sergeant who had set out for Niagara in the preceding April in quest of provisions and men was returning with both for the relief of the Fort, and they resolved upon the destruction of all. To that end they went and lay in ambush upon the shore of the lake where they could watch them pass. This sergeant, who did not know what had happened at the fort, because all was quiet when he left for Niagara, did not have any suspicions of the Indians and sailed along peacefully and without fear on the lake to Pine Point, forty-five miles from Detroit, where he camped for the night to do the cooking for the next day, following the custom of the *voyageurs*. The Indians who were hidden in the bushes and dense shrubs in that exact spot allowed them to disembark and pitch camp, and even to pass the night undisturbed. The people of the convoy, thinking themselves secure, were content merely to put a guard over the boats for fear the wind might come up in the night and set them adrift. All the others rested in peace.

The Indians, who were planning to attack them, did not sleep any during the night for fear their prey should escape them while they

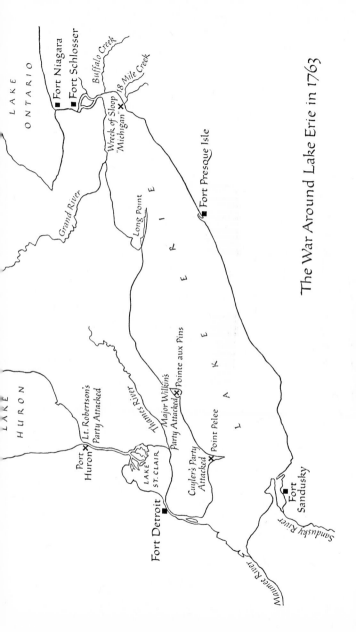

The War Around Lake Erie in 1763

slept. At daybreak they fell upon the voyagers, who were fast asleep.[56] Without giving them time to defend themselves they rushed upon the camp, massacred several, and made prisoners of the remainder, with the exception of thirty-five men and an officer who threw themselves almost naked into two barges and put out across the lake at a venture in the direction of Sandusky. All the remaining barges to the number of eighteen, and from twenty to thirty men,[57] fell

[56]Pine Point, present-day Point Pelee, some twenty-five miles east of the mouth of Detroit River, is the southernmost mainland extension of the Dominion of Canada. It is now a Dominion national park. Not far from its southerly extremity is a narrow place which serves as a short canoe portage—possibly the spot where the English were waylaid. The leader of the expedition was Lieutenant Abraham Cuyler of the Queen's Rangers, who was conducting a party of 96 soldiers (including, for some reason, a woman and a child) in ten bateaux laden with supplies from Niagara to Detroit. Having no knowledge of the Indian uprising, the detachment was easily surprised and overcome at the Point Pelee encampment the night of May 28–29. Peckham, who supplies a modern account of the disaster based upon Lieutenant Cuyler's own report, states that the attack was made soon after the landfall, the night of May 28. *Pontiac and the Indian Uprising*, 156–57. Lieutenant Cuyler's report, made to Lieutenant John Christie at Fort Presqu' Isle on June 3, states that the attack was made about eleven o'clock in the night of May 28. Printed in *Mich. Pioneer Colls.*, XIX, 188–89. Our Author mistakenly assumes that the sergeant was in charge of the detachment.

[57]Eight bateaux, instead of eighteen, were captured. The number of captives may have been larger. Of the 96

into the clutches of the savages, who brought them into the river to take them to Pontiac's camp by going up along the opposite shore, one after another, in a string.

In the first barge were four English soldiers and three Indians, and the other boats were manned about the same. Other Indians followed the barges along the shore uttering from time to time war-cries and yells of joy. When the four Englishmen came opposite the big vessel which was anchored in front of the Fort as a counter-defense, they undertook to escape in spite of the savages who were with them and the risk they were taking. They hoped that the crew of the sloop would notice their design and assist them, as was the case, and they turned straight toward her. When the Indians with them saw their prisoners' scheme they threw themselves upon them to make them take another course, but the Englishmen never wavered, keeping right on yelling to the vessel which at once replied with two cannon shots, one a ball at the Indians who were on land shooting at the escaping English in the boat, the other of grape-shot at the Indians who were in the stern of the barge.

men in Lieutenant Cuyler's detachment about 40 es-caped with him from the attack at Point Pelee. The re-maining 50-odd were either killed during the attack or brought as prisoners to Pontiac's camp.

The two shots produced the expected effect. The cannon-ball scattered the savages on the shore, and the grapeshot caused those on the barge to abandon it by jumping overboard to swim ashore. One of the three, as he leaped into the water, dragged an Englishman with him and both were drowned together. The other two gained the shore and seizing guns from their companions fired upon the escaping barge and slightly wounded a soldier in the right arm. The vessel fired two more shots at the Indians and drove them from the edge of the river; the three remaining soldiers with the barge reached the vessel with difficulty, badly used up, saving themselves and fourteen hundred pounds of flour, and a thousand pounds of bacon.

The rest of the Indians who had remained behind saw how the first barge with the soldiers had escaped in spite of the efforts of their companions, and they feared that the others would escape likewise. They decided on other means of getting to camp; landing, they tied their prisoners and led them in this way overland to the Ottawa village, and then carried them in canoes which their women had brought straight to Pontiac's camp. Upon their arrival here, following orders which they had received, they engaged in a butchery so bloody that the mere recital of it arouses as much horror as the spectacle itself.

This is the way it happened:

As soon as the canoes had landed in front of the camp the savages disembarked their prisoners, one company after another, upon the strand and made them strip naked, and other Indians then discharged their arrows into all parts of their bodies. Sometimes these poor unfortunates tried to pull back or lie down on the ground to avoid some arrow, but the Indians who were near made them get up by beating them with clubs and their fists. In order to satisfy these tigers thirsting for human blood, the poor victims had to keep standing till they fell dead in their tracks, and then those who had not engaged in killing fell upon the dead bodies and hacked them to pieces, cooked them, and feasted upon them. Some they treated with different cruelty, slashing them alive with gun-flints, stabbing them with spears, cutting off their hands and feet and letting them bathe in their own blood and die in agony; others were bound to stakes and burned by children in a slow fire.

There was no cruelty savagery could invent which these poor wretches did not suffer. At sight of the terrible spectacle one would have said that all the demons had been let loose upon these unhappy mortals. As a crowning wickedness, some of the dead bodies were left lying unburied along the way; others were cast into the river, which in this way received the last sad remnants of their rage. Even the Indian women took a hand, helping their husbands to glut themselves with the blood of these poor victims by likewise inflicting a thousand cruelties upon them. They vied with one another in seeing who could cause the greatest suffering; they slashed them with knife-cuts, as we do when we want to lard beef; and some of the women mutilated them to the point of emasculation. I could never finish if I wished to undertake it, the complete description of the cruel sacrifice and the sad end of all the unfortunates. However, there were some whose lives were saved by being adopted to work as slaves in the camp of the savages and witness the tyrannical death of their countrymen.[58]

After they had surrendered their prisoners to the Ottawas, the Hurons returned to join the guards of the captured barges, which they took to their own villages, along with the sergeant in charge of the convoy. They kept him with the intention of treating him as the Ottawas had

[58]The Gladwin manuscripts contain the narratives of James Connor and John Severings, soldiers of the Sixtieth Regiment, taken captive in May, apparently at the Point Pelee debacle, whose lives were spared and who were forced to work on the rafts built by the Indians to set fire to the *Michigan* and the *Huron*. See *Mich. Pioneer Colls.*, XXXVII, 649–52.

treated the others, and waited till dusk to take the barges to Pontiac, the great chief, so that he and all his band might share their prize.

The barges were loaded with powder and lead in bars, which was lucky for the Indians, who were running short. There were also flour and bacon, each barge carrying a ton of each, and liquor and fresh provisions for the officers of the Fort. The liquor caused great disorder in the camp; the savages got drunk and fought among themselves, and the taunts exchanged led to the death of two young braves the next day.

The Indian women, who understood the behavior of their men, hid their weapons while they were drinking for fear they would kill one another; and in order that the adopted prisoners should not suffer any they secreted them out of their husbands' sight. The chiefs, however, did not drink, and when they saw the disorder which the liquor caused in camp they knocked in the rest of the barrels and spilled the contents on the ground. In this way concord was restored.

Pontiac kept Campbell and McDougall, his two prisoners, under his eyes; through a ruse in the first days of the siege he had them hidden some distance away at the house of a French settler, under guard of ten reliable Indians, so that no harm should befall them.

May 31. Tuesday.

In spite of the precautions which Pontiac had taken against further disorder among his men by spilling the liquor, there was still enough of it left so that some Indians filled kettles to the brim with brandy and took them into the woods, where they could drink more at their ease during the night. Then they came back drunk to stir up quarrels with the young men by insulting them about the courage a good warrior ought to show; and these young braves, who were also under the influence of drink, were so aroused and puffed up with pride that they went recklessly to prove their courage and so met their death before the Fort.

Two of them ran up as if they would take the Fort themselves by assault; the sentries who were on guard above the north gate, when they saw them coming as hard as they could run, suspected that they had some evil design in view and fired down and mortally wounded both of them. One received a bullet which traversed his head from side to side, going in at the right eye and coming out on the left side above the jaw, and two buck shots through the body in two places; he dropped in his tracks, and was picked up by the soldiers of the garrison and brought to the Fort. Here he was exposed to public gaze as long as he remained alive from his wounds, and then buried in a corner of the bastion. The other savage, his companion, was shot twice through the body, and crawled away and died almost a fifth of a mile from the Fort. Other Indians carried him away and buried him near their camp.

The Indians of the camp, sick on account of their drinking of the day before, kept quiet the whole day and did not come to fire a single shot at the Fort.

A Frenchman who had stayed in the Fort to keep watch of a private house which was just outside, and who was getting tired of being shut up, was looking for some way to escape, but did not know how to do it. As he knew that the Commandant was casting about quietly for a trustworthy man to send to Niagara overland to warn the commander of that place of what was occurring here, he resolved to make himself of use to the officers under the pretext that he knew how to speak English a little, and in this way get a chance to go outside. To this end he relied upon the assistance of an English trader to whom he reported all that the other Frenchmen said among themselves. This trader, who had had several conversations with him in which he sounded him to the bottom, saw that he was a scoundrel and a traitor to his country, and would not present him to the Commandant.

Seeing that the trader did not listen to him and that he could not accomplish anything in this way, Luneau—this was the Frenchman's name—made use of the influence of a young woman who was intimate with the officers. This young woman whose name was Miss Des Rivières mentioned him to the Commandant, at the same time extolling his ability and making mention of the fact that he could speak English. The Commandant sent for him; he came, and without much examination was engaged upon the word of this young woman for the errand which the Commandant wanted done. He was equipped with all that he would need for the trip; and beginning with this day his pay was reckoned at six livres per day, to be given him upon his return. The same evening he received letters for Niagara, and in the night he departed and was rowed across the river by the soldiers. However, the scoundrel, instead of heading for Niagara when he landed, as he had led the officer to believe he would do, remained on the East Coast a whole day, divulging what was happening at the Fort. Next, he went down to the South Coast, where he spoke shamefully of the officers, and retailed a tissue of absurdities about the French who were in the fort. Several people, as soon as they saw he was a knave, threatened to take him and hand him over to the Fort for his just deserts; and fearing these threats might be carried out, he fled toward the

Illinois country in a couple of days and was never seen around Detroit again.

When the Commandant learned through the avowal of this young woman the same day that the Frenchman had already offered himself several times and had asked the trader to speak for him, he reprimanded the trader for not having done so. The trader offered as excuse that he did not know this man, and that he did not want to introduce him without knowing him well, because for such commissions one needed men who could be relied upon. As soon as the Commandant discovered the rascally trick which the Frenchman had played upon him, he praised the conduct of the trader and blamed the indiscreet zeal of the young woman; she was, so to speak, regarded by him with contempt, this being the proper reward which her work deserved.[59]

[59]The indiscreet lady may have been Angelique Des Rivières, who during 1763 acted as sponsor at several baptisms. Prior to 1771 she married Lieutenant Edward Abbott of the Royal Artillery Regiment. Their son, William George, was baptized Feb. 26, 1771. In the spring of 1777 Abbott was appointed lieutenant governor of Vincennes, being the first British officer at that post. Here he built Fort Sackville (captured by George Rogers Clark in 1779) but in February, 1778 he abandoned his post and returned to Detroit, giving as his excuse that he lacked means to supply the Indians with goods sufficient to keep them from joining the rebels, and he accordingly had left before they returned from their winter hunt. In July, 1778

June 1, Wednesday.

About two o'clock in the morning two soldiers and a trader who had been captured and adopted by the Indians escaped from their camp and reached the Fort. It was learned from them that Wasson,[60] the great chief of the Chippewas of Saginaw, had arrived the day before with two hundred savages of his band; and that immediately after his arrival at Pontiac's camp they had held a council and decided to harass the Fort no longer but to bar the approaches [from the East] so that no more assistance could reach the English, and to this end the Ottawas, Chippewas, Hurons, and Potawatomies were to depart this very day to go and prowl around the lake and capture the English they should find there.

he was sent to the West Indies and therewith ceased to figure in Detroit local history. Nor does Angelique appear further in the St. Anne Parish Register. Data adapted from sketch of Abbott's career in the present Editor's *The Capture of Old Vincennes* (Indianapolis, 1927), 54; entries in St. Anne Parish Register.

[60]Wasson (variously spelled) played a prominent role throughout the siege. In particular, it was he who killed Captain Donald Campbell on July 4 in revenge for the slaying of his nephew by a soldier. See *post.*, 175–76. About this time Wasson took a fancy to young John Rutherfurd, whom he obtained from Pontiac and kept for a time in his household, treating him with utmost kindness and planning to make him his son-in-law. Although his daughters were reckoned the handsomest "princesses" in the camp, Rutherfurd contrived to escape this destiny.

The thing which seemed to confirm what the prisoners had reported was that people saw passing behind the Fort through the woods something like three hundred men, who were going down to join the Potawatomies and Hurons encamped a mile and a quarter below the Fort, so that all could together go to scour the lake. Only the chiefs of each nation were left in camp to give their help to the young men who remained behind to guard the section around the Fort so the Englishmen could not get out to visit the surrounding coasts—a thing they had no desire to do, knowing full well it would not be good for them.

In the afternoon of the same day the Judge and the Commissary for the third time made a round of the French houses to collect food for subsistence till the return of the sloop, which was expected before long.

June 2. Thursday; Corpus Christi Day.

In the course of the afternoon some shots were fired by the savages who had stayed to watch the neighborhood of the Fort. However, it amounted to so little that the officers were content to observe them without returning the fire, seeing very well that it would be so much powder wasted.

In the night, around three o'clock in the morning, an English soldier who had been a prisoner of the Ottawas escaped from their camp and reached the Fort entirely naked. He brought a letter to the Commandant which Mr. Campbell, who was actually a prisoner in the camp, gave him for Mr. Gladwin. This letter had been found by the Hurons in the spoils of the leader [of a convoy] whom they had killed, and was brought into the camp to Pontiac. He gave it to Mr. Campbell to read, having Mr. La Butte, his interpreter, explain it to him. Mr. Campbell aided in the flight of the prisoner in order to enable the letter to reach Mr. Gladwin, Commandant of the Fort. It was written by an officer at Niagara to a friend of his in command at Miami, and in it he noted the conclusion of peace with all the circumstances. This was the occasion of a band concert in the evening to celebrate the good news.

June 3. Friday.

Except for those on guard around the Fort the Indians were quiet all day, as was their custom. About ten o'clock the Judge received orders from the Commandant to assemble all the French who were in the Fort to read to them the letter which he had received the day before by the prisoner who had escaped. This letter had been translated into French by a trader who spoke French well; it announced that peace had been declared between England and France, and by virtue of agreement made between the two crowns Canada, with all the Illinois country, remained in the hands of the English.

June 4. Saturday.

The Indians did on this day as on the preceding. About four o'clock in the afternoon the people of the Fort heard war-cries from the Indians who were returning by land on the other side of the river from the direction of the lake. No one knew exactly what these cries meant except that it was mistrusted the Indians had made some capture upon the lake.[61]

June 5. Sunday.

The Indians fired a few shots at the Fort merely to announce that they had not all departed for the lake, and that they did not intend to desist from their mad enterprise. The shots

[61]Later in the day it was learned that the Indians were celebrating the capture of Fort Miami on May 27. Ensign Robert Holmes was lured from the fort by his Indian mistress on pretense of visiting a sick squaw in a near-by cabin and shot down. The sergeant, who heard the shots, ran out to investigate and was seized by the Indians. The remaining eleven-man garrison closed the gates in readiness for defense, at which juncture Jacques Godfroy and Mini Chêne assumed the stellar role. En route to the Illinois with Pontiac's delegation they had waylaid John Welch, an English trader at Fort Miami, en route to Detroit with two boat-loads of peltry. The peltry, along with some of the prisoners, was sent back to Detroit in care of Beaubien, Chauvin, and Labadie, the remaining members of the delegation, while Godfroy and Chêne, together with their

did such little damage that the officers gave them no notice.

In the afternoon about two o'clock Indian war-cries, as on the preceding day, were heard on the other shore of the river. At these cries several persons mounted the sentry-walks to discover what it was. A number of savages were seen,—some on foot, some on horseback, uttering yells of victory and joy; others were bringing up two barges with merchandise and the traders which they had captured upon the lake, going up along the shore on the other side of the river with their prisoners. The sloop, thinking to make them abandon their prizes, fired several cannon shots at them, but they were too high or too

Indian companions, continued on to Fort Miami, carrying Welch and several of the men along to "make soup" of them on arrival at the Illinois. At the fort they caused Welch to be brought forward, who offered the soldiers within the alternative of mercy if they would surrender or death if they resisted. Upon consultation the leaderless soldiers yielded; several of them were carried prisoners to Detroit; the fate of the others remains unknown. Welch was also carried to Detroit, where he was presently murdered by the Ottawas. The informant, whose credibility was certified by James Sterling and Sampson Fleming, further related that when Isidore Chêne, Mini's brother, heard of the report he burst into tears, exclaiming that he "wished to God his brother might die in that place (Fort Miami) for as soon as he arrived at Detroit he would be hanged." *Mich. Pioneer Colls.*, XXVII, 632–33; Hough, *Diary of the Siege of Detroit,* 22, 26; Peckham, *Pontiac and the Indian Uprising,* 160–61.

low, and the savages jeered and went on with their capture to Pontiac's camp.

June 6, Monday.

The weather, a little dark and even rainy, caused the Indians to be content to hover around the neighborhood of the Fort without firing a shot. On the other hand, others went to the homes of the settlers to procure provisions, which were voluntarily surrendered. This did not prevent the savages from constantly harming them by killing oxen, cows, or swine, and even in their cornfields which they spoiled by their going and coming; they did not dare pass along the main road for fear of the large sloop which sent a cannon ball as soon as anyone was visible.

June 7. Tuesday.

The Indians, who had not fired a shot for two or three days and were getting tired of not using powder, came and kept up a fusillade upon the Fort from ten in the morning till seven at night. As they had neither barns nor any other buildings to hide behind and shelter their approach, they fired from behind the bluff, and frequently from within the woods which were almost seven hundred yards distant from the Fort, and separated by the hill in such a way that their shots sometimes passed over the Fort. Other Indians were concealed farther away along the fences around the fields of the settlers, or in the farm buildings often beyond the range of the sentries' guns, because of the hidden defenses which protected the three principal sides of the Fort. About seven o'clock they ceased firing and withdrew, as satisfied as when they began.

June 8. Wednesday.

About eight o'clock in the morning the Indians came to commence firing. It appeared, as will be seen, that when they began the action they intended to keep it up for some time, but a slight rain changed their minds and compelled them to retire to their camp. They left guards only, according to their custom, to see that nobody went out or came in who might be an obstacle to them. Still, there were always some persons going and coming, but these were respected among the Indians who did not have any distrust of them.

In the afternoon the officers were warned by a resident of the region that the Indians planned to make an assault during the night under cover of the storm. The officers, who had become acquainted with the strategy of the savages since the beginning of hostilities, replied that they were ready for them. They thought that this pretended enterprise would end like the others; but since distrust is the mother of security, in order not to be surprised they were on their guard with the troops the whole night long, which passed as quietly as if they had been in their beds. At sunset three war-cries were heard in the direction of the Huron village, but no one knew what it meant.

June 9. Thursday; Little Corpus Christi Day. The Indians, who kept up their firing through impetuosity only, were quite tranquil all day. Toward three o'clock in the afternoon thirteen war-cries were heard on the other side of the river, and the curiosity of a good many English and French was aroused; they mounted to the top of the stockade to discover the cause of it. One could see a large number of Indians on horseback and on foot, running about uttering war-whoops and yells of joy, and firing upon the big sloop which was anchored in front of the Fort; one could also see other Indians who were coming by water along the land with three barges and some prisoners that they had captured upon the lake. These Indians were a part of those who had gone to watch the lake. When they passed in front of the sloop, she fired at them five cannon shots of grape and ball which wounded some without hindering them from continuing their course.

Around evening of the same day it was learned through a Frenchman that the remainder of the band of Sekahos, chief of the Chippewas of the Thames River, had arrived during the preceding night, and that they numbered 45 men. With the coming of this last band the savages numbered 850, all actually in camp or around the lake, and all of different nations and under different chiefs; there were 250 Ottawas under Pontiac; 150 Potawatomies under Ninivois; 50 Hurons governed by Takay; 250 Chippewas under Wasson; 170 of the Chippewas under Sekahos; all of whom were under the authority of Pontiac, their over-chief. They would all have been good dogs if they had wanted to bite.

June 10. Friday.

The Indians, who had remained in the camp the day preceding, received news from the Hurons, who arrived from hunting in the woods back of little Lake Sandusky, that the officer who had escaped with his thirty-five men was among the Sandusky islands.[62] Pontiac said they must be caught so they should not carry the news to Niagara, and he detached fifty men from those of his camp; they passed in the rear of the Fort to go and notify the three hundred who had set out on the first of June to scour the lake, and were to join themselves to them to capture the officer. Fortunately, before the last

[62]The officer was Lieutenant Abraham Cuyler, who with a remnant of his command had escaped from the Indians at the Point Pelee attack on May 28. He had crossed the lake to Fort Sandusky, to find it in ruins, and had then continued on to Fort Presque Isle (present-day Erie, Penn.), where he arrived on June 3.

forty joined the others the officer had left the islands with his two barges and taken route for Niagara along the south side of the lake.

The Potawatomies of St. Joseph, who had attacked the English and had taken possession of the fort[63] there by killing part of the garrison and making prisoners of the others, had left the fort in charge of the French settlers of that locality, and come with their prisoners who numbered seven, including the commander, to join the Potawatomies of Detroit.[64] They reached the

---

[63]Fort St. Joseph at present-day Niles, Michigan was garrisoned by fifteen soldiers under the command of Ensign Francis Schlosser "a very young man too fond of his liquor." Peckham, *Pontiac and the Indian Uprising*, 90. On May 25 Potawatomi chief Washee entered the fort with a swarm of followers on the pretext of seeking an interview with the Commandant. Schlosser was seized, all but six of the soldiers were killed "in about two minutes," and the fort was plundered. Schlosser and the other survivors were carried to Detroit where the officer and the soldiers were exchanged for a prisoner held by Gladwin on June 15. St. Joseph was one of the earliest French settlements in the interior of the Continent. Although the fort was never restored after its destruction in 1763, the settlement has remained continuous until the present day. For interesting data concerning it in the French period see "The St. Joseph Baptismal Register," edited by Rev. George Paré and the present Editor, in *Mississippi Valley Hist. Rev.*, XIII, 201–39 (Sept. 1926). Schlosser's report of the massacre is printed in *Mich. Pioneer Colls.*, XXVII, 636–37.

[64]The fort was left in charge of Louis Chevalier, trader, who had resided at St. Joseph since about the year 1745

village the preceding night. When they learned
that the English held two savages of their nation
prisoners in the Fort, they came about four
o'clock P. M. with a certain Mr. Gamelin to the
foot of the Fort to enter into negotiations with
the Commandant concerning the exchange of the
officer who commanded at St. Joseph for the two
Indians in the Fort.[65] The proposition did not
suit the Commandant, who wanted the Potawatomies to surrender all their seven prisoners
for the two Indians. The latter would not consent to this exchange and returned as they had

and had acquired a position of influence over the natives
of the adjacent area. For many years thereafter Chevalier
continued to represent the government in the conduct of
affairs at St. Joseph. In 1780, however, Lieutenant-
Governor Sinclair of Mackinac, suspecting the loyalty of
the inhabitants of the village, ordered their wholesale
removal to Mackinac, where they would be remote from
the rebel influence. Among the deported were Chevalier
and his seventy-year-old wife, who were compelled to
abandon all of their property comprising "ten houses,
good lands, orchards, gardens, cattle, furniture, utensils,
and debts." Imprisoned for a time at Mackinac, and with
all his papers confiscated, Chevalier was presently allowed
to journey to Detroit, whence he appealed to Governor
Haldimand of Canada for permission to return to St.
Joseph to salvage his abandoned property. See *Mich.
Pioneer Colls.*, XIII, 61–63; entries in the St. Joseph
Baptismal Register, in *Miss. Valley Hist. Rev.* XIII, 201–39.

[65]The founder of the American line of Gamelin was
Michael Gamelin *dit* Lafontaine, a native of St. Aubin in
the diocese of Blois, France. He became a surgeon and
migrated to Canada where in 1663 he married Margaret

come, deferring until the following day the conclusion of the exchange.

June 11. Saturday.

There still remained in the vicinity [of the Fort] one house and a shop which the fire had not been able to reach because of their remoteness somewhat from the others, which served as a shelter for the Indians. An officer at the head of twenty men made a sortie to burn them and clear the plain. When he returned from this excursion the same officer had his men empty and clean out the boats and barges, which were beached in front of the Fort, and put them into condition for service in case the sloop which had left for Niagara did not return. If they should see themselves compelled by shortness of provisions to abandon the post, these boats with the

Crevier, a native of the diocese of La Rochelle and widow of Jacques Fournier. Their grandson, Laurence Eustache Gamelin, was born in Lower Canada in 1704 and prior to 1741 migrated to Detroit. In 1740 he married Marie Joseph Dudevoir *dit* Lachine and by 1759 had sired a dozen children. He was engaged in trade, and in 1755 was a captain of militia. On May 1, 1747 he received from the Government a grant of land immediately east of the town which is now known as the Brush farm, or Private Claim No. 1. He subsequently sold this land and in 1757 was living at the Coast of the Potawatomies, a fact suggestive of his serving as spokesman for the tribe. He was buried at Detroit on March 7, 1771. His widow was buried on Jan. 10, 1803. Data adapted from Denissen, Detroit Genealogies (Ms.).

large sloop would serve for them to fall back upon Niagara. The savages did not fire at all during the day.

This same day Mr. Lacelle, Jr., arrived from Montreal with two canoe-loads of merchandise and liquor which he unloaded at Widow Gervaise's[66] to keep it from the clutches of the Indians, but he was "sold" and the Potawatomies came and demanded some of it, threatening to plunder him if he did not share with them. To get rid of them he surrendered two barrels of wine.

Pontiac learned of this arrival almost as soon as the Potawatomies; he knew that they had taken the liquor, and fearing that he would not get his share he crossed the river with his chiefs, visited Lacelle, and ordered him to move his liquor up to the house of Jacques Campau,[67]

[66]Jean Gervaise, a native of France, born in 1621, migrated to Canada, where he was appointed to the office of Fiscal Procurator. On Feb. 3, 1654 he married Anne Archambault at Montreal. Their grandson, Louis Gervaise, was born at Montreal, April 12, 1708. He married there, on Feb. 18, 1737, Marie Madelaine Langlois, who had been born at Detroit on Aug. 19, 1711. Gervaise was a trader and a captain of militia who lived at the South Coast of Detroit (Sandwich). He was buried at Detroit on Feb. 7, 1763. "Widow Gervaise", who survived him but a few months, was buried on Oct. 29, 1763. Data adapted from Denissen, Detroit Genealogies (Ms.).

[67]The Campau family, one of Detroit's oldest, is still numerously represented there. Its first Detroit progenitor was Jacques Campau, who was born and married at

near his camp. The goods were taken unharmed to the home of Mr. Labadie, Lacelle's uncle.[68]

When Mr. Lacelle was induced to change his quarters Pontiac gave him to understand that being near his camp he would not be disturbed because he, Pontiac, would answer for his

Montreal and who removed with his family to Detroit in 1708. He followed the trade of toolsmith. In 1734 he obtained a grant of land lying between Mt. Elliott and Beaufait avenues, now known as Private Claim No. 18, or the Meldrum farm. In keeping with his time he sired a large family.

His grandson, Jacques, the person here noted, was born March 30, 1735. On August 17, 1761 he married Catherine Menard. She died about 1781 or 1782, and on Jan. 5, 1784 Jacques married (second) Marie Françoise Navarre the widow of Lieutenant George McDougall, first owner of Hog Island. He acquired a farm extending westward from Chene Street toward St. Aubin which is now known as Private Claims Nos. 91 and 14. It was in his house that Major Robert Rogers sought refuge during the battle of Bloody Run. Parkman, who has vividly described the scene, mistakenly characterizes Campau as "old" and "gray." In fact he was twenty-eight years old and had been married but two years. He became an officer of militia of the Northeast Coast, and in 1770 was treasurer of St. Anne's Church. He was buried at Detroit June 23, 1805. Data adapted from Denissen, Detroit genealogies (Ms.) and sketches in *The John Askin Papers*, I, 33 and 48–49.

[68]The Lacelles of Detroit and vicinity were descended from Jacques Lacelle, a carpenter, who was born in the Diocese of Paris in 1670. He migrated to Canada and on August 8, 1698 married at Montreal, Angelica Gibaut. They had several children, all of whom, with the possible exception of Jacques, the eldest son, migrated to Detroit,

people;[69] however, to have peace, he handed over five barrels and the savages left him alone.

The Potawatomies, who had come the day before to effect an exchange of prisoners, came back this day at four o'clock, but returned no better off than they had come, reaching no more of a settlement this second time than the first.

---

where one of the daughters married Pierre Descomps *dit* Labadie. The trader who now arrived at Detroit was Jacques Lacelle III, a grandson of the original immigrant, and, as our Author states, a nephew of Pierre Labadie. Lacelle was born at Montreal, May 1, 1735. On Feb. 18, 1765 he married at Lachine, Teresa Berthelet *dit* Savoyard. Soon afterward he settled at Detroit, where he continued to engage in the Indian trade, operating particularly on the Maumee and its adjacent area. Prior to 1776 he located at Miamitown (Fort Wayne, Indiana) where one or more of his children were born. The family fled the place in advance of La Balme's invasion of 1780, taking refuge, apparently, at Detroit. Here Jacques was buried, Aug. 14, 1791. Three of his sons, Jacques, Antoine, and Francis, were prominent early-day settlers of Monroe. Data adapted from sketch in *The John Askin Papers*, I, 197.

[69]There was good reason for this, since Labadie was one of the more ardent supporters of Pontiac. A somewhat gory tale, related long afterward by James Knaggs, suggests this relationship. The narrator received it, in turn, from his father, Whitmore Knaggs, who was born at Fort Miami in 1763 and who married Marie Joseph Descomps *dit* Labadie at Detroit, June 23, 1797. The story related that following the defeat of Captain Dalyell, Pontiac invited the leading French residents to partake of a grand feast in celebration of the victory. After it was over he inquired of Labadie (one of the guests) "How did

June 12. Sunday.

The day passed very quietly at the Fort without any action on either side. Toward ten o'clock in the morning Mr. Cavelier reached the house of Widow Gervaise with canoes loaded with wine and goods for the place, and from him it was learned that there was an abundance of all sorts of merchandise and provisions in Montreal at a low price. Around three o'clock P. M. the guards of the sloop brought to shore the dead bodies of several persons whom the Indians had massacred the day before; they were buried on the strand opposite the Fort.[70]

June 13. Monday.

Rainy weather all day kept both sides from firing.

June 14. Tuesday.

The day was like the preceding one up to four

you like the meat? It was very good young beef, was it not? Come, I will show you what you have eaten." Suiting the action to the word, he drew forth from a sack which was lying on the ground behind him the bloody head of an English soldier. Holding it up by the hair, he said, "There's the young beef." Although the disclosure turned Labadie's stomach, he subsequently described the "young beef" as very tender and quite appetizing until Pontiac's revelation was made. See Friend Palmer, *Early Days in Detroit* (Detroit, 1906), 370–71.

[70] Five bodies were picked up according to Lieutenant Hay, two of them recognizable, the rest "so mangled that it was impossible for anybody to have the least knowledge of them." Hough, *Diary of the Siege of Detroit,* 23–24.

in the afternoon when the Indians fired a few shots which did not receive the least attention from the English. During the day the Indians visited Mr. Cavelier to get some liquor. He refused, whereupon the savages became enraged and plundered his whole stock of liquor, merchandise, and even the provisions he had brought for his return trip because he knew very well that provisions would cost more here than in Montreal.

June 15. Wednesday.

The Indians, who as a usual thing are not very forehanded unless compelled by circumstances, had run out of the provisions which they had captured with the barges of the convoy, and they had to depend upon the French settlers to live until they could take others. In addition to what was given them they also killed the stock of the settlers.

Along toward ten o'clock in the forenoon the Potawatomies came for the third time to make an exchange of prisoners and gave the Commandant of St. Joseph and two soldiers for one of the Indian prisoners held by the English. They were disappointed in the exchange because they demanded the Indian named Big Ears, who was greatly esteemed among them, and they received one by the name of No-Kaming whom they regarded as a rogue. But the disappointment was due to No-Kaming himself, who told the Commandant not to give the Potawatomies the one of the two they asked for, but to give them himself instead, because the Potawatomies had no regard for him; and since the other was a man of prominence in the nation, if he was kept, the Potawatomies who wanted him would raise their offer and give all the prisoners. The advice, although coming from a savage, was accepted as good and he was given in exchange, and Big Ears was kept so as to obtain with him the other prisoners. But the Potawatomies were hardly satisfied with their negotiations, finding themselves frustrated in their hopes.

June 16. Thursday.

The Indians were very quiet the whole day. Since it is a practice in all places besieged or blockaded by an enemy that silence be observed, and there be no ringing of church bells for any necessity whatever, so that the enemy may not know the hours when the public frequent church, for that reason the bell of the parish church of this place had not sounded for any service since the commencement of the siege. When the Commandant learned from the Curate the reason for this he gave permission to ring the bells for all the needs of the church, and it began its function at noon by sounding the Angelus.

About three o'clock P. M. the chiefs of the

good Huron band, who had not taken any part in hostilities since Father Potier, in order to restrain them, had refused them the sacrament, came for a parley. They entered the Fort by a false gate and discussed terms of peace with the Commandant, making many excuses for what they had done. The Commandant listened to them and gave them a flag, which they accepted in sign of union, and they departed without any other conclusion than the flag.

June 17. Friday.

The day passed without any movement on the part of the Indians. Notwithstanding they had decided in council on the seventeenth of the previous month not to allow anyone from the outside to enter the Fort, still there were some favored ones who had liberty to come and go in order to watch over their affairs on both sides of the river as necessity demanded. Through one of these the Commandant learned that the sloop was in the lake off the entrance to the river, and had been seen by a man named Repus, an Indian slave, who had been hunting in that quarter. When the sloop departed the Commandant had told its commander that as soon as he should learn of his return to the river he would have a cannon fired in order to tell him by this signal that he and his troops were still in the Fort. The Commandant did this at the first news; he

ordered two cannon shots fired at sunset to
notify the sloop that she could come up and that
he, the Commandant, was still master of the Fort
and neighborhood.

June 18. Saturday.

An inhabitant of the East Coast opposite the
Fort crossed the river about two in the morning
to bring the Commandant certain news about
the sloop. This led him to order the cannon by
the southeast gate to fire twice at different inter-
vals as a signal; the order was executed at five
A. M.

At noon of the same day Father Du Jaunay,[71]
the Jesuit missionary of the Ottawas from
Michilimackinac, arrived with seven Indians of
this nation and eight Chippewas of the same

[71]Father Pierre Du Jaunay S.J. came to the western
mission in 1735, and continued his missionary labors until 1765, when he was recalled to Quebec, where he served
as spiritual director of the Ursulines until his death,
June 16, 1780. He officiated at the St. Joseph Mission
(Niles, Michigan) at various times from 1738–52 and was
stationed among the Ottawas of L'Arbre Croche (near
Harbor Springs, Michigan) from 1742 until his withdrawal in 1765. He wielded much influence over his
charges and was instrumental in effecting the release of
the survivors of the massacre of Mackinac, June 2, 1763.
His present errand to Detroit was as bearer of a letter from
Captain Etherington of Mackinac conveying news of the
massacre there and appealing to Major Gladwin for help.
This appeal Gladwin, of course, was in no position to com-
ply with. Du Jaunay, whom Etherington characterized as

place in command of Kinonchamek, son of the great chief of the nation.[72] They brought news of the defeat of the English at this post on the second of the month by the Chippewas. The Jesuit father was lodged with his colleague, the missionary to the Hurons.

June 19. Sunday.

The Fort was not molested; the arrival of the son of the great chief the day before caused a suspension of hostilities between the savages and the Fort. He located his camp in a meadow two miles and a half above the Fort, a mile and a quarter above Pontiac's camp. The Indians in

"a very good man," remained several days at Detroit, during which he vainly appealed to Pontiac to release his English captives. See George Paré, *The Catholic Church in Detroit,* 1701–1888, index entries. On the downfall of Mackinac, see Alexander Henry's vivid narrative in his *Travels and Adventures,* (the Lakeside Classics, Chicago, 1921.) It is interesting to observe that our own Author gives the correct date of the massacre—June 2—which Henry incorrectly associated with King George's birthday, June 4. The letter of Captain Etherington to Major Gladwin which Father Du Jaunay bore to Detroit is printed in *Wis. Hist. Colls.,* VII, 162–63.

[72]The father of Kinonchamek was Minavavana or Le Grand Saulteur, who figures interestingly in Alexander Henry's *Travels and Adventures,* dealing with the massacre of Mackinac, June 2, 1763. Minavavana, although critical of Pontiac's conduct, was a friend of the French and an ally of Pontiac. Following the assassination of the latter in 1769, Minavavana journeyed from Mackinac to Cahokia to avenge his death. See Peckham, *Pontiac and the Indian Uprising,* 316.

camp went up to see him land and welcome him in the name of their chief; they were received pretty coldly and told that in the afternoon he and his followers would come to see Pontiac and hold a council. At this news Pontiac ordered all the Indians of each nation to remain in their lodges all day to hear the words of the great chief of the Chippewas by the mouth of his son.

While they were getting ready for the council there arrived at the Huron village toward ten o'clock in the morning two canoes of Shawnees and Delawares from the Ohio River who came to see what was going on. Upon their arrival they learned of the coming of Kinonchamek and of the location of his camp; they did not disembark, but went straight to his camp to hold a council concerning what was taking place here. Two or three Frenchmen were called to give information about matters since the beginning of the siege by the Indians, and concerning all that had been done by Pontiac's orders, after which they were sent home.

Around two o'clock P. M. Kinonchamek, followed by his men and the Shawnees and Delawares, came to Pontiac's camp to hold a council as he had had announced the night before. Upon his arrival all the chiefs assembled and grouped themselves in silence, after their custom, in a sort of circle. When each Indian had taken his place,

Kinonchamek arose and spoke in the name of his father, addressing himself to Pontiac:

"We have learned at home, my brothers, that you are waging war very differently from us. Like you, we have undertaken to chase the English out of our territory and we have succeeded. And we did it without glutting ourselves with their blood after we had taken them, as you have done; we surprised them while playing a game of lacrosse, at a time when they were unsuspecting. Our brothers, the French, knew nothing of our plan. The English found out that they were the ones we had a grudge against; they surrendered. We made prisoners of them and sent them unharmed to their Father in Montreal. The soldiers tried to defend their leaders; we killed them, but it was done in battle. We did not do any harm to the French, as you are doing; on the contrary, we made them guardians and custodians of our captives."

[More directly to Pontiac]:

"But as for thee, thou hast taken prisoners upon the lake and the river, and after having brought them to thy camp thou hast killed them, and drunk their blood, and eaten their flesh. Is the flesh of men good for food? One eats only the flesh of deer and other animals which the Master of Life has placed on the earth. Moreover, in making war upon the English thou hast made war upon the French by killing their stock and devouring their provisions, and if they refuse thee anything thou hast had thy followers pillage them. We have not done so; we did not rely upon provisions from the French to make war; we took care when planning to attack the English to lay in provisions for ourselves, our wives, and our children. If thou hadst done likewise, thou wouldst not be in danger of incurring the reproaches of our Great Father when he shall come. Thou awaitest him, and we too, but he will be satisfied with us and not with thee."

Pontiac in the face of this speech was like a child surprised in some fault with no excuse to give, and he did not know what to say. As soon as Kinonchamek had finished speaking, the chief of the Eries spoke for his band and for the Delawares:

"My brothers, we have also fallen upon the English because the Master of Life by one of our brother Delawares told us to do so, but he forbade us to attack our brothers, the French, and thou hast done so. Is this what we had told thee by means of the wampum belts which we have sent thee? Ask our brothers, the Delawares, what the Master of Life had told to them: it is all right to kill during battle, but afterwards, and when one has taken prisoners, it is no longer of any value; nor is it to drink the blood or eat the flesh of men. Since thou art French as well as we, ask our brothers, the French, if, when they are making war and have taken prisoners, they kill those whom they have brought home with them. No, they do not, but they keep them to exchange for their own men who are prisoners among the enemy. We see well what has obliged thee to do what thou hast done to our brothers, the French: it is because thou hast begun the war ill-advisedly and art now in a rage at not having been able to take the English in the Fort thou art bound to have our brothers, the French, feel thy bad humor. We desired to come to thy assistance but shall not do so, because thou wouldst say that all the harm which thou and thy followers have caused our brothers, the French, was caused by us. For this reason we do not desire to put ourselves in a bad light with our Great Father."

During the whole council and even afterwards Pontiac did not say a word, even though well aware of his fault, and Kinonchamek, the Eries, and the Delawares withdrew without receiving any reply from him, and returned to their camp to rest.

About three in the afternoon it was learned that the English at Miami had been defeated and the post plundered.[73] Toward seven in the eve-

[73]Fort Miami was captured on May 27, and the news of the capture was learned at Detroit as early as June 4. The

ning news came that a large party of Indians had ascended the river to Turkey Island, opposite the place where the sloop was anchored. When the people on the sloop detected the great movement among the savages on the island they feared that they were about to make an attempt to capture them; to avoid this danger they raised anchor and retired to the open lake where they could wait for a suitable wind to ascend the river without risk.

June 20. Monday.

About ten A. M. the Indians came to fire a few rounds at the Fort from the north side, and after this fusillade the English perceived that the Indians came along the highway insolently and fearlessly. To break them of their boldness a loophole was cut through the palisade on that side to mount a cannon which should sweep the suburbs and put a stop to the movements of the Indians.

Around four o'clock in the afternoon the news came that Presqu'Isle and Beef River, posts originally established by the French, but for three years now held by the English, had been captured by the Indians. As the rumor was not confirmed, it remained uncertain.[74]

entry in our Author's narrative at this point seems evidently misplaced.

[74]Fort Presqu'Isle at present-day Erie, Penn., was built by the French in 1753 and abandoned by them on

On the initiative of Father Du Jaunay a council was held between him and Pontiac concerning the liberty of the English.

June 21. Tuesday.

From break of day a great movement was discerned among the natives, who did nothing but pass and repass behind the Fort, at the same time whooping as if they had some attack in mind. These operations, which seemed a little peculiar, led the English to watch them and keep on their guard all day long. Although they tried to discover the cause they did not learn it till the following night when Mr. Baby came at two

---

Aug. 13, 1759. The English now occupied the place until its capture by the Indians, following a three-day siege, on June 22, 1763. Obviously the news could not have reached Detroit on June 20. Lieutenant Hay reports it as being received on June 29. Hough, *Diary of the Siege of Detroit*, 36. Fort Le Boeuf (at Waterford, Penn.), a minor work garrisoned by thirteen soldiers, was attacked by the Indians and abandoned by its garrison on June 18.

Although Lieutenant Christie, Commandant of Fort Presqu'Isle, had conducted a desperate defense before surrendering, Colonel Bouquet, upon hearing the news, expressed the hope that Christie had been killed. The Indians had agreed that the garrison should be allowed to retire to Fort Pitt, but once in control they promptly violated the agreement and carried the inmates into captivity. Lieutenant Christie, along with a woman and four soldiers, was taken by the Hurons to their village at Detroit, where two of the soldiers were slaughtered; Christie, the woman, and one soldier were delivered to Major Gladwin on July 9.

o'clock in the morning to tell the Commandant
that several French settlers, who lived at the
lower part of the South Coast upon the edge of the
river had told him that they had seen the sloop;
she seemed well laden and had many people in
her, and this same news which the savages had
learned first had put them in commotion.[75]   At

[75]The American progenitor of the Baby family was
Jacques Baby, born in France in 1633, who came to
Canada as a member of the famous Carignan Regiment,
sent by Louis XIV to defend the colony against the Iroquois. In 1670 he married Jane Dandonneau of Three
Rivers. He fathered twelve children, the last one, Raymond Baby, being born posthumously Dec. 16, 1688.
Jacques Baby had engaged in the Indian trade, and
Raymond followed the same calling. He was in Detroit
as early as 1716 when he witnessed the baptism of two
savages. His son, Jacques Baby *dit* Duperon, or Jacques
Duperon Baby, our present subject, was born Jan. 4,
1731. He grew up habituated to the wilderness and during
the Seven Years' War distinguished himself, along with
three of his brothers, as a leader of Indian war parties in
forays along the upper Ohio frontier. Meanwhile a young
Virginian named George Washington was vainly endeavoring to protect the Virginia portion of the same
frontier from Indian massacres and in frustration expressed his willingness to sacrifice his own life if by so
doing he could save the harassed settlers.
On several occasions during the course of the war
Jacques Duperon Baby was sent to Detroit, and he is
supposed to have been the spokesman for the French
inhabitants in negotiating the surrender of November 29,
1760. However this may be, it is certain that he settled
here upon, or before, the close of the war. On November
23, 1760 he married Susanne Réaume. In 1762 and 1763

this recital of Mr. Baby, the Commandant again ordered that two cannon be fired suddenly at daylight in the direction of the southwest to warn the sloop.

June 22. Wednesday.

The Indians, who had received news of the sloop, as I have just related, did not come around the Fort to annoy it. This favorable time was utilized to employ the garrison with throwing down and burning the rest of the fences around the gardens, cutting down the fruit trees, and removing from around the Fort whatever could offer any shelter to an Indian. In the course of the day the news of the taking of Presqu'-

---

they were living in the Fauburg Ste. Rosalie on Detroit's South Coast (modern Sandwich), but during the siege they moved into the Fort, where they continued to reside. Following his change of allegiance Baby loyally supported the British government and throughout the siege of 1763 he afforded material aid to the garrison. During the years from 1761 to 1789 twenty-two children were born to Jacques and Susanne Baby. Several daughters married British army officers and three sons became officers in the army, one of whom attained the rank of major general. Another son studied medicine at the University of Edinburgh. Still another, Jacques Baby II, who was born during the siege, August 25, 1763, became a prominent Canadian official. The Baby mansion in Windsor, now the home of the Windsor Historical Society, was being erected by him when the War of 1812 opened and it was successively utilized as headquarters by General Hull and General Harrison. See sketches in *The John Askin Papers*, I, 292-93 and family data in Denissen, Detroit genealogies (Ms.).

Isle was confirmed, because the savages who had undertaken this expedition were seen returning in large numbers, bringing back with them by land the prisoners which they had taken; among these were the Commandant of the place and a woman, both of whom were presented to the Hurons.

About three o'clock the Commandant received information concerning the cargo of the sloop and the number of people aboard; at four o'clock the Commissary and the Judge visited the French households to seize provisions for the fourth time. Kinonchamek departed for Michillimacinac.

June 23. Thursday.

The Indians did not come to fire on the Fort during the day, as they were occupied with a project for the capture of the sloop, which they knew to be at the mouth of the river. Early in the morning they passed in large numbers in the rear of the Fort to go to join those who had left two days before; they all collected on Turkey Island, which is a sort of narrow strait because at this point the river is very narrow. The Indians had constructed on the island an entrenchment with tree trunks which they had felled and piled upon the shore of the river on the side where the sloop had to pass. They also heaped up earth and strengthened it with branches in such a way that if they were seen in their fortifications they had nothing to fear from balls. In this retreat they waited the coming of the sloop.

About six o'clock in the evening the wind seemed to have become favorable for ascending the river and the occupants of the vessel lifted anchor to take advantage of it. When it was opposite the island the wind fell and they had to anchor, in ignorance of the ambuscade which had been laid for them on the island. The Indians waited till night to attack, but those on board, anticipating that they would not reach the Fort unmolested, were on their guard with lookouts fore and aft, determined to sell their lives dearly.

In their entrenchment the Indians, from the moment the vessel had anchored across from them, had not ceased to study the number of men in her, and seeing only twelve or fifteen persons they believed that they could attack without any risk. However, there were sixty or seventy men aboard. During the day the Captain had hidden sixty men in the hold, for he suspected that the Indians who were constantly prowling about would venture an attack if they saw only a dozen men.[76] And this was the case. Between eight

[76]He was bringing in reinforcements of supplies and men from Niagara for the relief of the Detroit garrison. The attack was made in the night of June 23.

and nine o'clock in the evening the Indians put
out in their canoes to surround the sloop and
board her. A sentinel on the forecastle saw them
coming in the distance; for fear of being heard
they were paddling very slowly. The commander of the sloop was warned, and he had all
his men come quickly and quietly on deck and
take places along the gunwale with weapons in
their hands; in silence, all ready, with cannon
loaded, they were ordered to wait for the signal
which was a hammer-blow on the poop. Thus
prepared, they allowed the enemy to come within
gunshot.

The Indians were overjoyed at the silence
which reigned on the vessel and thought that
there were actually only twelve men on board,
but a moment later they were greatly undeceived;
for when they were within gunshot the signal
was given and there was a general discharge of
cannon and guns which swept through the savages who returned to their entrenchment quicker
than they had come, with a loss of fourteen men
killed and as many wounded. They no longer
had any desire to approach near the sloop, but
they fired at her all night from their breastwork
and wounded two men. The next day for lack of
wind the vessel dropped down into the lake to
await a favorable wind with which to come up.

June 24. Friday.

The Fort was quite unmolested the whole day. The Indians who were all the while occupied with the scheme of taking the sloop had forgotten the Fort for some time. There were only prowlers around the Fort, two of whom came in their defiance so near that they were seen. Twenty men with an officer at their head sallied out to capture them, but the two savages discovered them and seeing that the twenty men were after them they dropped their plan very quickly and took to their heels; the English came back as they went out—with nothing.

June 25. Saturday.

The weather remained unsettled all day and there was no hostility on either side.

June 26. Sunday[77].

Several soldiers, who had passed the night on the bastions as usual, brought word to the Commandant that they had seen two Indians enter a house in the vicinity, five hundred yards north-

[77]Lieutenant Hay records that Pontiac attended mass at the Huron Mission, after which he impressed three "chairs," or two-wheeled gigs for himself and his attendants to ride in while they conducted a search for provisions. He gave the settlers whose cattle he seized birch-bark bills of credit signed with his mark, the figure of a raccoon, drawn at the top of each. The goods were taken to the house of Meloche, where Antoine Cuillerier acted as Commissary. Hough, *Diary of the Siege of Detroit,* 34–35; Peckham, *Pontiac and the Indian Uprising,* 190.

east of the Fort. At four in the morning, by order from the Commandant, Mr. Hopkins made a sortie at the head of twenty-four men picked from his company to surround the house and take them prisoners. When they reached the place the two savages were not there,—only the caretaker. They searched the house everywhere in the belief that the two Indians were hidden, but they found only two sows with their litters, which they took and brought into the Fort instead of the Indians. In some measure this capture was worth more than the prize they wished to make.

The same day about ten in the morning two Indians who had seen from a distance how a couple of soldiers had fastened out the horses of two officers, their masters, came sneaking up through the tall grass, cut the ropes and drove the animals away.

June 27. Monday.

The Indians, according to their custom, prowled around the Fort all day without doing any firing. Since Mr. Campbell and Mr. McDougall had been prisoners in Pontiac's camp, Mr. Gamelin had visited them every two days and sometimes every day; today at three o'clock P. M. he brought a letter to the Commandant which Pontiac had dictated and caused Mr. Campbell to write; in it Pontiac notified the Commandant that he and his whole force must evacuate the

Fort at once, because he expected within ten days Kinonchamek and the great chief of the Chippewas with eight hundred warriors of his nation whom he would not be able to control, and as soon as they arrived they would capture the Fort. To this the Commandant replied that he was ready for them, and him, too, and defied them.[78] This reply did not please Pontiac nor his savages, but the English cared very little about that.

Toward eight o'clock in the evening it was learned indirectly that the sloop had hoisted anchor preparatory to coming up the river.

June 28. Tuesday.

A part of the Indians who had gone down the river to capture the sloop came back to camp after having failed, fortunately; as they passed the Fort they saluted it with a volley without harming anybody. About two P. M. the Hurons re-entered their village. The news that the sloop had lifted anchor turned out to be true; when the wind had veered into the southwest the ves-

[78]In his reply to Pontiac, Gladwin stated that until Lieutenant McDougall and Captain Campbell were released he would engage in no further discussions. To which Pontiac, nothing daunted, rejoined that he had too great regard for the two officers than to send them into the Fort, since the kettle was already on the fire and he would be obliged to boil them with the rest. Hough, *Diary of the Siege of Detroit,* 35.

sel took advantage of it and sailed out of the evil spot and came up as far as the River Rouge,[79] two and a half miles distant from the Fort, where she anchored, when the wind failed, a little below in plain sight of the Fort. At seven o'clock in the evening two cannon shots were fired as a signal to her, but there was no reply; this aroused forebodings, for people thought the Indians had captured her by a second attack. This was the view expressed quite loudly by the Judge, but it did not prevent the English officers from celebrating with the band in the bastion which faced the side where she was anchored.

June 29. Wednesday; St. Peter's Day.

The Indians did not fire upon the Fort at all during the day; some of them rested, while others collected to make a descent upon the French settlers to recoup themselves for their wasted labors. About three P. M. some twenty war cries were heard behind the Fort; they came from the savages who were returning from the capture of Fort Presqu'Isle.

The sloop remained at anchor all day where she had stopped the day before for lack of wind.

June 30. Thursday.

The Indians were quiet all day expecting reinforcements.

[79]Site of the vast present-day Ford Motor Company plant.

Around three o'clock in the morning three war-whoops and some yells of joy were heard coming from the Indians, but no one could discover what it meant.

When the southeast wind came up those on the sloop lifted anchor to take advantage of it. As they passed the Huron village they saw the savages standing with folded arms, wrapped in their blankets, at the doors of their cabins; the sloop fired a broadside of grape-shot and ball which wounded some and made all hurry into their cabins. Some of the Indians seized their guns and followed the sloop, firing upon her till she came safely to anchor in front of the Fort at four P. M. On board were the thirty-five men and the officer who had made their escape toward Sandusky, as I have mentioned before[80]. This officer came ashore to bring some letters to the Commandant in which mention was made that peace had been declared and Canada remained in the possession of the English and his Britannic Majesty paid all expenses which had been incurred in Canada since the commencement of the war.

July 1. Friday.

The Indians, who prowled constantly around the outskirts of the Fort and the homes of the

[80]Lieutenant Abraham Cuyler, for whose disaster at Point Pelee on May 28 see *ante,* 110–11.

settlers, frightened the domestic animals in the region; one herd of three oxen, three cows, and two calves came into the Fort; they belonged to Mr. Cuillerier.

Mr. St. Martin, interpreter for the Hurons since the beginning of the siege, had abandoned his house which is about a quarter of a mile southwest of the Fort, because the Indians took refuge behind it from which to shoot. This led the English to fire upon it, and since he was no safer in the house from the Indians than from the English he retired to the missionary, Father Potier's, to remain till the end of this affair. The day before he had an interview with a Huron who was loyal to him and told him that the Indians wanted to make the French take up arms against the English; he was not in a mood to consent to this, and asked of the Commandant a refuge in the Fort for himself and family, which was granted. He came with his mother-in-law, his wife, and all his dependents. He lived one day with Mr. La Butte and afterwards at the house of Mr. Bellestre.

July 2. Saturday.

Mr. McDougall, who accompanied Mr. Campbell when they left the Fort to visit the Indian camp and had been kept a prisoner, escaped along with three other Englishmen, also prisoners at the camp; they reached the Fort at three o'clock in the morning. When they fled from the camp they did all they could to bring Mr. Campbell with them, but to no avail; he would have liked to follow them, but he was shortsighted and feared that in running from one danger he would rush headlong into another which might end his days before his time. He did not want to run any chances of dying till he had to.

At five in the morning an officer made a sortie with twenty men to destroy the fences of Mr. St. Martin's garden and cut down the grain in which the savages hid. When the latter saw that their hiding places were being cut down and destroyed, they started with determination in pursuit of the English who went back to the Fort quicker than they had left it. * * * * * The Indians kept up a fire upon the Fort without injuring anybody. In the meantime the English have been content to keep close watch every day, and have placed soldiers on guard in two temporary bastions which are outside on a slope of the hill behind the Fort; during these days there are always four sentries in each bastion day and night.

The garrison and the new arrivals from the sloop were busy unloading her a part of the day, and fetching the cargo into the warehouse.

Toward seven o'clock in the evening news came that the Indians had been to the homes of all the French settlers in every neighborhood, and had brought to their camps all the old men and heads of families to take part in a council which they desired to hold, and in which they wished to compel the French to take up arms against the English. In the course of the night it was learned that the Indians after the council I am going to speak about had sent back all the fathers of families and the old men to their homes without doing them any harm.

Pontiac, who was in despair over the arrival of the sloop, resolved to cause the French settlers by force or friendship to take up hostilities, seeing that in spite of the designs of himself and his followers reinforcements of men and provisions reached the English. In order to succeed in his project he had all the heads of families and the old men summoned to a council in his camp, under the pretext that it was about a matter they were concerned in. When all had arrived, following his usual custom he began to speak, addressing himself to the French and at the same time handing them war-belts. This is what he said:

"My brothers, I am getting tired of seeing our lands encumbered by this carrion flesh [the English], and I hope you feel the same. I believe you are about ready to conspire with us to destroy them; still, it has seemed to me that you have been abetting them to our hurt. I have already told you, and I say it again, that when I began this war it was for your interest as well as ours. I knew what I was about.

"I know Fort Erie has fallen. I say I know it, and this year all the English in Canada, no matter how large their force, must perish. It is the Master of Life who commands it. He has made known his will unto us,—we have responded, and must carry out what He has said, and you French, you who know Him better than we,—will you all go against His will? [Up to now] I have not wished to speak, hoping that you would let us take our course. I have not wished to urge you to take up arms with us against them, for I did not think you would side against us. I know very well you are going to say that you do not side with them, but you are siding with them when you report to them all that we do and say. For this reason there is only one way open today: either remain French as we are, or altogether English as they are. If you are French, accept this war-belt for yourselves, or your young men, and join us; if you are English we declare war upon you, which will show our valor all the more because we know you to be children of our Great Father [the king of France] as well as we; to make war upon our brothers for the sake of such dogs pains us, and it will cost us an effort to at-

tack you inasmuch as we are all French together;
and if we should attack we should no longer be
French. But since we are French it is wholly the
interests of our Father, yours and ours, that we
defend. Therefore answer, my brothers, that we
may come to an understanding; and behold this
belt which makes its appeal to you or your
young men."

One of the principal Frenchmen[81], who had
almost suspected the design of Pontiac and had
brought with him to the council a copy of the
Capitulation of Montreal and Detroit, arose and
responding for all the French said, holding the
document in his hand:

"My brothers, your wishes are sufficiently
known to us. When you began this war upon the
English we foresaw that you would force us to
take up arms against them. We do not hesitate
an instant to follow you and with you defend the
interests of our Father, but first you must remove, if you can, the bonds which tie our hands
and which the Father of the French and the

---

[81]Probably this was Robert Navarre. Lieutenant Hay
records that on July 4 Navarre published the Articles of
Peace to the French and the Indians. Hough, *Diary of the
Siege of Detroit*, 40. It seems probable that the date of
Pontiac's Council with the French settlers (July 2) is the
correct one. Major Gladwin had received the news of the
Peace Treaty as early as June 2. See *ante*, 123;
Hough, *Diary of the Siege of Detroit*, 19.

Father of the English have knotted about us as the only hindrance to our accepting this war-belt. Do you think, my brothers, that it is very easy or agreeable for us to see you take up our interests without assisting you? Believe us, we are grieved over it, and you forget what we said on this subject in the last council which we all held together. But the King of France when he gave these lands here to the King of England commanded us not to fight against the English, but to regard them as our brothers and the English father and king as our father and king. You believe, possibly, that we say this out of lack of desire. No! Our Father has made known his will to us by sending us this document and he orders us to remain quiet in our houses, for he alone wishes to deliver us. Without considering this you say that if we do not accept your war-belt you will make war upon us. * * * Our Father has not forbidden us to fight when our brothers, the English, attack us; although you have called us English it will not be of our own desire if we shall fight against you. But Frenchmen, as we are now and have always been, we are surprised, my brothers; you forget that when our Father [the French commandant] left here you promised him you would defend us, our wives and our children, and it is not so. What harm have we done you as far as the English are concerned? And then did you not promise our Father that you would wait for him to come back? And you have not done so, because you are fighting instead of waiting for him. * * * * and when he comes he will deliver us, and we shall join ourselves to him and all do his will. It is now your turn to speak, my brothers!"

Pontiac was spurred on by a band of irresponsible and vagabond Frenchmen who had neither chick nor child in the region, and had thrown off the mask, inasmuch as they did not have much to lose; he replied that it was necessary to do as he did, and if it was not the old men, then it must be the young men. When the French saw themselves driven into a corner by the obstinacy of Pontiac they asked him for delay until the following day, when all would return bringing their reply.

One of the leaders of the renegade French[82], who thought that by putting himself and his whole gang on the side of the savages they would

[82]Apparently this was Zachariah Cicotte. On Dec. 24, 1763 Louis Jadot affirmed to Major Gladwin that Cicotte told Pontiac that they would not fight with him against the English, since in the event of failure their wives and children would be exposed to inevitable ruin; but that there were 300 young men in the settlement who had neither parents nor property to lose, who might and ought to join him, and a plan was laid to attack the fort about July 5, the Indians to assail it from without while the French inside would rise against the garrison. The deponent further affirmed that Cicotte, Antoine Cuillerier,

be safe in their foolishness, arose in his place, at the same time picking up the belt, and turning to the Indians said:

"I and my young men break away from our bonds; we all accept the war belt which you offer us and are ready to follow you. We shall go and find other young men to join us,—there are enough of them—and we shall make them * * * * * that you may see how soon we shall capture the Fort and all that is in it."

All the old men who had been called to the council trembled when they saw such a base proposal made by people without heart or honor; they asked to be allowed to make their reply on the next day, and very much grieved to see a band of scoundrels espouse Pontiac's cause they asked permission to withdraw.

Pontiac dismissed the old men, shaking hands with them all, and each went home filled with

Mini Chêne, and others had known in advance of Pontiac's plan to slaughter the garrison in the Council of May 7. See Jadot's declaration in *Mich. Pioneer Colls.*, XXVII, 656.

For sketch of the Cicotte family line see *The John Askin Papers*, I, 36. Zachariah, born in 1708, married at Detroit on January 8, 1736 Marie Angelica Godfroy. They had ten children in the following years. For many years Zachariah Cicotte lived in the Fort and engaged in trade. On April 1, 1750 he obtained a grant of land 3 arpents by 40 extending westward from present-day Wabash Street and legally known as Private Claim No. 726. He settled on this farm in 1762 and remained on it until his death. He was buried Aug. 11, 1775.

anger at having been a witness of an action so despicable which sooner or later would involve all the French. The vagabonds who had accepted the belt remained at the camp, for they well knew that after such a deed they would not find anyone who would receive them into his home. The council was not concluded till eight o'clock, which made it too late to find out what warlike qualities these new-made savages possessed.

July 3. Sunday.

The Indians spent the whole day in festivities, regaling their new warriors. The Commandant, who learned in the morning what had taken place the night before in the camp, ordered the Judge to count the guns, weapons, axes, and pick-axes of all the Frenchmen in the Fort, and to make a list of those who had arms and of those who had none, so that in case of need everything could be made use of.

Toward ten o'clock A. M. a sortie was made by twenty men for the purpose of destroying a fence which enclosed an orchard. The trees were cut down and the palings pulled up and burned with the trees, and the field was cleared. The garden belonged to Mr. Cesir, a French citizen of the Fort[83]. In the afternoon the Commandant

[83]Jean Cesire, a blacksmith, born at Lachine, Jan. 26, 1698, migrated to Detroit prior to the year 1735. He was buried April 23, 1767. His wife, Margaret Charlotte

ordered the Judge to call all the French in the Fort together at the church door in order to read the news of the conclusion of peace. After the reading the band played for an hour.

A son of one of the settlers was unhappily among the plotters, but by a multitude of remonstrances and a feeling of shame he was induced to recognize his fault and that of his companions and desert them. He brought away with him the war-belt which he gave to his father to take back to Pontiac. Early in the morning the father went to see Pontiac, who loved him greatly, and said to him:

"My brother, thou who art chief whom up to now I have known as possessing sense, but thou hast it no longer since thou dost listen to young men who will betray thee instead of aiding thee and perhaps will deliver thee to the English. Thou who dost command so many people, thou allowest thyself to be commanded by people who have no intelligence. Those who have told thee that they are going to assist thee in capturing the Fort will be the first to run away. Thou hast always scorned a man who placed himself * * * * * * * * saying to thyself that he was a worthless fellow, and today * * * * * * Hast thou lost thy mind? Why place * * * * * like

Girard, was buried Sept. 28, 1797. Denissen, Detroit Genealogies (Ms.).

thee, young men who have no sense and who are going to come here in tears to deny what they have said? * * * * * with thee, because they will kill thee perhaps. O Indians, you are men and have no need of anybody and if you make use of these young men, under what obligations will our Father be to you? When he comes and learns how you have compelled the French to take up arms he will say: 'It is not you who have driven out the English, it is the French and the rest of you have only looked on.' He will scorn you. Therefore, Pontiac, listen to me. Take back thy war-belt which my son returns, and ponder well what I have just told thee."

Pontiac, for an Indian, was not lacking in intelligence * * * * * as well as those of his Ottawa nation. [He listened] very attentively to what the Frenchman had just told him. "Thou art right, my brother," he replied, "and I thank thee for the warning thou hast given me." And he took the war-belt and they separated—one to go to the camp, the other to his home. From this time on [the Ottawas] did not press the French to take up hostilities. It was only the Chippewas, the Potawatomies, and the bad Huron band that tried several times to compel the French to attack the English, as I shall tell later.

The heads of families replied to Pontiac's council that they did not wish to take up arms.

When the Hurons of the bad band, who were never of any value either to the English or the French, knew that Pontiac had contented himself with volunteers and did not care, anyhow, to urge the French to begin hostilities, they leagued together with the Potawatomies and the Chippewas to force the settlers to join them; they threatened to attack them if they did not consent, and said they would lead away the young men in spite of their fathers. This caused a great deal of bad blood between the French and the Indians; the French wished to remain neutral, but fearing that the threats of the three nations would be followed by action they seized their arms for mutual defense, kept guard, and posted sentries on the highways for fear of surprise.

When the savages saw that the French were on their guard they did not dare attack them, but took their revenge on the live stock which they found scattered around. Mr. Pierre Réaume[84],

[84]René Réaume, born in the bishopric of La Rochelle in 1643, married Marie Chevreau, who was born in 1652. Their son Pierre, born July 28, 1698, settled at Detroit in 1722. Another Pierre Réaume, a grandson of René Réaume and Marie Chevreau, who was born at Lachine on Oct. 6, 1709, is our present subject. On Jan. 20, 1738 he married at Detroit Susanne Hubert *dit* la Croix, a native of Montreal. One of their daughters, Charlotte Réaume, who was born at Detroit on June 18, 1738, married Pierre Charles Daneau du May, son of a former commandant of Detroit, on Nov. 4, 1760. Another daughter, Susanne,

who lived on the other side of the river across from the Fort and feared that this storm might chance to fall on him, came to ask the Commandant for an asylum in the Fort, and it was granted him.

July 4. Monday.

Mr. Pierre Réaume who had received permission the night before to retire into the Fort with his whole family brought over the river in the early dawn of the morning his household goods and animals, and went to lodge in the house of Mr. Dequindre[85] which was vacant at the time.

became the bride three weeks later of Jacques Duperon Baby. Still another daughter, Veronica, who was born Feb. 2, 1745, on July 26, 1764 married, at Father Potier's Church of the Hurons in Sandwich, Judge Gabriel Christopher Legrand, for whom see *ante,* 89. The youngest daughter, Marie Louise Réaume, born March 8, 1750, on July 16, 1770 married at Assumption, Sandwich, Alexis Cuillerier *dit* Beaubien, whose father was Antoine Cuillerier *dit* Beaubien, ardent supporter and favorite of Pontiac. For the Réaume family history see *The John Askin Papers,* I, index entries, and Denissen, Detroit Genealogies (Ms.).

[85]The founder of the Dequindre line in America was Michael Dagneau de Douville, Sieur de Quindre, an officer in the French army. He married Marie Lamy at Sorel, May 16, 1688 and one of their sons, Louis Cesaire Dagneau de Quindre, born at Sorel on Oct. 8, 1704, is the subject of our present sketch. On Dec. 4, 1736 he married at Montreal Marie Anne Picoté de Bellestre, daughter of François Marie Picoté de Bellestre and Marie Catherine Trotier *dit* Beaubien. Bellestre was an army officer, and a brother-in-law of Alphonse de Tonty, second com-

The Commandant learned that the Indians, with some of the renegades, had thrown up an entrenchment in the night in the rear of the house of Mr. Baby northeast of the Fort * * * * * distant. Hereupon he ordered Mr. Hay, officer of the Royal Americans, to sally forth with thirty men to level the nightly work of the savages and vagabonds.

As much to reconnoiter as to carry out the Commandant's orders the scouting party, who were [not aware that] the Indians were waiting in

mandant of Detroit. Bellestre was stationed at Detroit for many years prior to his death, Oct. 9, 1729, and at various times he served as acting-commandant during temporary absences of Tonty. His second wife, Marie Catherine Trotier, whom he married in 1710, left Montreal for Detroit in the spring of 1729. The family she brought to Detroit eventually adopted the surname of Beaubien, giving rise to the far-flung Beaubien line, which is still represented in Detroit. One son was Antoine Cuillerier *dit* Beaubien, prime favorite of Pontiac during the siege of 1763. He was born at Montreal, March 22, 1697 and was therefore sixty-six years old at this time. Another son, Jean Baptiste, on May 30, 1740 obtained a grant of land east of the Fort which is now known as the Beaubien farm, a portion of Private Claim No. 2. In 1760 he was a captain of militia. A daughter of Antoine Cuillerier *dit* Beaubien, Marie Anne, born April 19, 1730, married the interpreter, Pierre Chêne *dit* La Butte, who, unlike his father-in-law, was firmly loyal to Major Gladwin throughout the siege. In the C. M. Burton edition of the Pontiac Journal, the wife of Louis Cesaire Dequindre is mistakenly identified (p. 204) as the daughter of François de Bellestre, the last French commandant of Detroit.

ambush, advanced at double quick toward the trench. Just as they were on the point of reaching it the savages and renegades showed themselves and opened fire without wounding anybody. Mr. Hay was not disconcerted but animated his men by his example [to advance toward] the enemy, and charged on in the face of the fire.[86] * * * * * the victory remained in doubt. Hearing the firing, the Commandant mounted the ramparts and after he had studied the situation, fearful that other Indians would reinforce their comrades and imperil his scouting party, he quickly ordered out relief for Mr. Hay. Capt. Hopkins at the head of forty troops and

[86]Concerning this spirited engagement Hay himself merely recorded: "This morning early made a Sortie with twenty Men to cover a party to bring in some Powder and Lead that was in Mr. Babie's House, after which we destroyed an Entrenchment that the Indians had made, from which they annoyed us. The Indians being advertis'd that we was out came down and Capt. Hopkins was sent out with twenty Men more who with nine or ten Frenchmen and the Party that was first out, pursued them as far as it was safe; we took one Scalp and wounded two or three more, we had one Man wounded." It is one of the ironies of history that to Hay fell the distinction of being branded as a coward by George Rogers Clark at the taking of Vincennes in 1779. Yet in comparison with Hay, Clark was himself a mere novice in the conduct of Indian warfare. See Hough, *Diary of the Siege of Detroit*, 39–40, and M.M. Quaife, "Detroit Biographies; Jehu Hay," in *Burton Hist. Coll. Leaflet*, VIII, 1–16 (September, 1929).

some French of * * * * * hastened out on the run.

The savages held their ground against the first comers because they were entrenched, but with the coming of the reinforcement they found themselves too weak. The renegades abandoned the breastwork at once and fled, and it was only the Indians who disputed the field for some time with the English, who carried the place. When Mr. Hopkins saw the obstinacy of the Indians he ordered a part of his men to deploy in a circle in order to take the Indians on the flank, while the rest occupied them in front. This maneuver succeeded. The Indians abandoned their shelter and were pursued so closely that in the retreat two of them were killed, one of whom was scalped by an Englishman who had formerly been a prisoner among them. A soldier was slightly wounded by a blow on the head from the butt of a gun in the hands of one of the Indians who was killed. As this same man killed the Indian he got all of his silver ornaments to pay for the damage. After the Indians were driven away the trench was filled up and all the fences near by were burned.

When the expedition was finished the whole troop re-entered the Fort with the French whom the Commandant called together on the parade-ground to thank for the way they had seconded his men, and also to inquire which of them had no arms. Weapons were brought out and given to these, and any who had arms which were faulty in any particular were directed to carry them to the royal warehouse, where they could be repaired at the King's expense. And * * * to choose whether to volunteer or to elect an officer to command them as need might be. They chose Mr. Sterling for their leader, and accompanied by an officer they all went to his house, where the Judge notified him that the French militia had elected him to command them and how he was appointed captain.[87] This honest man thanked the men for their choice and said he hoped there would never be any occasion for them to regret it. They all withdrew well pleased and quite resolved to do their duty under the command of such a leader.

About four o'clock in the afternoon an officer who had commanded the fort at Sandusky and been taken prisoner by the Indians escaped from

[87]For James Sterling, see *ante*, xxviii–xxix. Posthumous fame has been conferred upon him by the legend that Pontiac's plot to destroy the garrison was revealed to him by his sweetheart, Angelique Cuillerier, moved by the desire to save her lover's life. During the American Revolution he was accused of disloyalty and Lieutenant-Governor Hamilton had him arrested and deported to Lower Canada. Information concerning his subsequent career has not been found. Data adapted from sketch in *The John Askin Papers*, I, 47.

their camp, or rather from a French farm house where his [Indian] wife had sent him for safe-keeping.[88] It was learned from him that the Indian who had been shot and scalped was a Chippewa chief and nephew of Wasson, chief of the Saginaw Chippewas, and that Wasson, enraged that his nephew had been killed in the skirmish of the morning, went to Pontiac's camp, said abusive things and demanded Mr. Campbell for revenge, saying: "My brother, I am fond of this carrion flesh which thou guardest. I wish some in my turn,—give it to me."

Pontiac gave him up and Wasson brought him to his camp, where he had his young men strip him of his clothes. Then he killed him with a blow of his tomahawk, and afterwards cast him into the river; the body floated downstream to

[88]That is, for protection from abuse or slaughter by the Indians. The officer was Ensign Christopher Pauli, Commandant of Fort Sandusky and lone survivor of the massacre of its garrison on May 16. Brought to Detroit as a prisoner and forced to run the gantlet, he was saved from further mistreatment by a squaw who claimed him for her husband, as related by our Author, *ante,* 104. According to Rutherfurd's narrative he was aided in his escape by a handsome young squaw who had fallen in love with him. Lieutenant Hay records that upon entering the fort, "dressed like an Indian, his Hair being cut and painted in their Fashion," no one recognized him. See Hough, *Diary of the Siege of Detroit,* 40, and Pauli's own account of the massacre at Fort Sandusky, in *Mich. Pioneer Colls.,* XXVII, 636.

the place where the Frenchmen had taken him
when he left the Fort,—in front of Mr. Cuillerier's house, and here it was buried.[89]

Around six o'clock in the evening powder and
balls were delivered at Mr. Sterling's house for
the needs of the French militia.

July 5. Tuesday.

The Indians did not disturb the Fort at all.
They visited the settlers and took the axes and
pickaxes which they could get hold of and carried them to the blacksmiths to have them
sharpened. The smiths refused to work for them,
saying their forges were in the Fort.

The same day the leader of the renegades, now
living with the Indians, undertook to enlist the

---

[89]They "strip[p]ed him, and carried him to their camp,
where they killed him, took out his heart and eat it
reaking from his Body, cut off his Head, and the rest of
his Body they divided into Small Pieces," Lieutenant
Hay, *Diary of the Siege of Detroit,* 41. Young John Rutherfurd, whom friendly Indians saved from sharing Captain
Campbell's fate, soon afterward was conducted by his
captors past "a dead body, mangled and scalped, which
the dogs were eating ... It was a shocking spectacle—
the head scalped, the nose, arms, ears and legs with other
parts of the body cut off," which the Indians told him
was the mortal remains of Captain Campbell. See his
Narrative, *post*. The *Gentleman's Magazine* (London) for
September, 1763 published a short account of the war in
America based upon reports in the American papers. In
it Detroit is identified as "on the Illinois," and the Indians are reported to have given Captain Campbell "time
to pray" before proceeding to slaughter him.

services of the sons of the settlers to help him capture or burn one of the sloops. To this end he visited some of the settlers where he knew there were young men to try to enroll them in his gang. But it was known that his plan had miscarried and he resolved to abandon it. In order to escape [the renegade fled] to the Illinois country, for many of the settlers threatened to hand him over to the Commandant, who would not have been slow in rewarding him according to his just deserts.

July 6. Wednesday.

The Indians for some days had cherished the idea of burning the big sloop which guarded the highway and hindered them from approaching the Fort from that side; they did not know how to go about it and visited several French settlers to inquire in what way they could do it. In order to get rid of them and be let alone, the only reply the settlers made was that they did not know how to undertake the matter.

July 7. Thursday.

The Indians were quiet enough as far as the Fort was concerned for the Commandant and his officers gave them something to do in their camp. This was the way of it: Early in the morning there arose a slight wind from the southeast which appeared to favor the English in their design to pay Pontiac a visit in his camp with the big sloop.

As they were getting under way the wind fell and they anchored until it should become more favorable. The wind was not long in rising; by eleven o'clock it had increased and grown strong enough for them to weigh anchor a second time, and now not uselessly. They ascended the river to a point in front of Pontiac's camp where they anchored and lavishly saluted his village with cannon balls and grenades.

Neither Pontiac nor his people were expecting such a visit, but they were able to save themselves by flight, abandoning their cabins and belongings which were knocked over by the balls and shells. This pastime lasted from noon till * * * The sloop remained at anchor till four o'clock when she returned to where she came from. With all this destruction not a savage was wounded.

During the time that a part of the English were visiting Pontiac's camp with terror, the Potawatomies came with Mr. Gamelin for the purpose of making peace with the Commandant; their request was granted on condition that they would remain neutral and surrender their prisoners—a promise they made but did not keep.

The same day both the Huron bands held a council between themselves with the object of coming to the Fort to make peace with the Commandant.

July 8. Friday.

The Commandant, who had a plan to send the sloop to Niagara, ordered that she be ballasted by demolishing an old building which formerly served as a powder magazine to get stone to load her with. This was done in the course of the morning by the French and the soldiers.

Toward two o'clock in the afternoon the Hurons came to treat with the Commandant in accordance with the council they had held in their village the night before. At the Commandant's order the gate was opened for them and they were admitted into the Fort; they held a council on the parade-ground and asked for an opportunity to make peace with the English. They were told that if they would return all the prisoners and merchandise in their lodges all their errors would be pardoned and the past forgotten. They said they wished to return to their village and make the same announcement to their brothers and get them to consent; they then withdrew, willing to do all that was required.

About five o'clock the Potawatomies returned with Mr. Gamelin and promised to give up the English prisoners who had been in their village for several days in exchange for their comrades who were held here.

Around six o'clock the Ottawas took up a position in ambush in the rear of Mr. Beaubien's house,[90] and for an hour fired upon the big sloop which replied with several volleys without harming them in the least.

This same day Mr. Maisonville arrived with a cargo of brandy, lead, salt, and bales, and reached * * * with great difficulty.[91]

[90]The house of Antoine Cuillerier *dit* Beaubien.

[91]The Maisonville family is one of the oldest in the Detroit River area, having representatives here from 1703 to the present time. It is descended from Robert Rivard *dit* Loranger, a native of France, who migrated to Canada and in 1664 married Magdelene Guillet, a native of Three Rivers. They lived, and are buried at Batiscan. Their children, ten in number, went by various surnames. The tenth child, René Alexis Rivard *dit* Loranger, born at Batiscan, July 10, 1691, was the father of Alexis Loranger *dit* Maisonville and Joseph Loranger *dit* Maisonville, both of whom migrated from their native Batiscan to Detroit. Identification of the individual here noted is uncertain. Captain Hay records that he was at Ouiatanon (present-day Lafayette, Indiana), when that place was taken (on June 1) and that he brought with him into the Fort five boat loads of peltry and lead weighing 10,000 pounds. Hough, *Diary of the Siege of Detroit,* 44. Although this would have been a rich prize for the Indians Maisonville "being resolute and acquainted with their manner and customs" eluded them. James Sterling reported in a letter of Feb. 26, 1765 that Maisonville had just returned from a mission to the Indians of the Illinois and characterized him as "a very sensible fellow" well acquainted with the country. Two Maisonville brothers (precise identity again uncertain) figured tragically in the Vincennes campaign of 1778–79. One of them supplied Lieutenant Governor Henry Hamilton with advance information concerning the route and other conditions, and accompanied him on the campaign. The other, François Maisonville,

July 9. Saturday.

The Ottawas and the Chippewas formed a scheme to burn the sloops at anchor if they could. To accomplish their purpose they set to work to make a fire-raft which they intended, when all was ready, to send down the river with the current to the vicinity of the big sloop. This task kept them busy two days, during which time the Fort was not annoyed.

The Hurons, as they had promised the day before, came about four o'clock bringing with them seven prisoners—five men, one of whom was the commandant of Presqu'Isle,[92] a woman, and a child; they handed these over to the Commandant and asked to make peace. They were told in reply that they must return all the merchandise which they had taken from the traders, even to a needle, and then terms of peace would

"a famous Indian partisan", was captured by Clark, who ordered him put to death. A soldier, commanded to scalp him, reluctantly began the operation, when the brother interceded with Clark and persuaded him to desist. However, borne to imprisonment in Williamsburg, Virginia, he found relief from the hardships imposed upon him by committing suicide. Data adapted from Denissen, *Detroit Genealogies* (Ms.); *The John Askin Papers*, I, 325; Hamilton's narrative of the Vincennes campaign in M.M. Quaife, *The Capture of Old Vincennes* (Indianapolis, 1927), index entries.

[92]Lieut. John Christie, for whom see *ante*, 147. Another prisoner was Chapman Abraham, for whose capture see *ante*, 74.

be granted them. They withdrew, promising to restore all the merchandise they had in their village.

Toward seven o'clock in the evening the Commandant was warned that the savages would fire the Fort by means of arrows, and that they had made a fire-raft out of boats with which to set fire to the two sloops in the course of the night. It was true that they were working upon a plan to burn the sloops, but it did not succeed.

July 10. Sunday.

The Indians, who had worked for two days to set fire to the vessels, about two o'clock in the morning sent down their work which was two boats bound together with ropes and filled with kindling of dry wood and [birch bark]. The whole thing burst into flame and came floating down the river, passing two hundred feet from the sloops without doing them any harm at all. When the Indians saw that their time was lost

With him another Jewish trader, Gorsed Levy was captured. In the division of the spoils Abraham fell to the Potawatomies and Levy to the Miamis. Lieutenant Hay records that the latter, on June 10 sought to surrender Levy to Major Gladwin in exchange for a certain quantity of goods. They were rebuffed, however, and the next day it was reported that they had "gone off" with him. On Dec. 30, 1763 Levy, along with several other traders, signed a petition to General Gage concerning losses they had sustained at the hands of the Indians. Hough, *Diary of the Siege of Detroit*, 45–46, 224–25.

with the useless work they set about another fire-boat and left the Fort in peace the whole day.

About seven in the evening the Commandant was warned by the French from outside that the Indians were surely going to set fire to the Fort under cover of the night. However this might be, he put no credence in it for generally these news-bearers were liars who invented many things or told some lie or other for sake of the welcome, and then came and troubled the officers, who frequently laughed at them for their pains. Still, as it frequently happens that some truth is concealed among a tissue of stories and lies, the Commandant gave orders that four Frenchmen and four soldiers be posted at once in bivouac a couple of hundred feet beyond the four corners of the Fort, with orders to fire if they saw anything and then fall back upon the Fort.

July 11. Monday.

The savages, who were occupied with a second enterprise about like the first, did not come to fire on the Fort the whole day.

Toward ten o'clock in the morning the Hurons came to fulfill their promise and brought all the merchandise which had been plundered from the traders upon the lake and on the river, and peace was concluded between them and the English.

About six a Frenchman from without the Fort came to warn the Commandant that the savages had the second fire-boat ready and that they would set it afloat in the night; which was done.

July 12. Tuesday.

One hour after midnight the Indians sent off their second raft with as much success as the first one. Two cannon shots were fired from the Fort toward the highway leading off to the southwest which scattered the savages, who were seated at the edge of the river to admire the effect of their work. The sloop fired two cannon shots at the raft and broke it to pieces, and rendered the labor of the natives useless.

About ten o'clock in the morning the Potawatomies came in accordance with their arrangement to fetch three English prisoners and make peace, which was granted them. They then demanded their man. The Commandant told them that when they had returned all the prisoners which they had in their village they would get the man they wanted and everything would be settled. They put off till three the settling of what was asked of them. Toward three in the afternoon the sloop which had come from Niagara set out on her return, with orders to bring back provisions and reinforcements.

About the same time the Potawatomies returned as they had promised in the morning with seven prisoners whom they surrendered to the Commandant, at the same time asking for their comrade. As he was about to hand him over a man named Jacqueman[93], one of the Potawatomies' recent prisoners who had been given to them for a present, said to the Commandant in English that they had still other prisoners in their village. This led the Commandant to change his mind and hold back the prisoner, telling the Potawatomies to bring all the prisoners they had and their request would be granted. This did not please them much, and with an interchange of glances they formed the plan at the risk of destruction to fall upon the Commandant and the officers who were with him and kill them. The thing that arrested the deed was this: an Ottawa Indian who entered the Fort with the others and had been recognized by Mr. McDougall for an Ottawa was arrested and locked up under a heavy guard. Although displeased not to obtain their demands, this frightened the Potawatomies and they withdrew with the determination to wreak vengeance in the coming night.

July 13. Wednesday.

The Indians, who had learned some days before that guards had been posted outside the Fort to surprise them if they came near the Fort in the night, resolved to be revenged for the refusal they had received the day preceding. To this end, they came in the night to spy out the

[93]Chapman Abraham.

sentinels, who were ordered to fire at whatever they saw; the Indians discovered and fired upon them and dangerously wounded a Frenchman who was posted on the southwest side. The rest of the day passed quietly enough around the Fort.

The same day in the afternoon the Hurons asked for a secret council. There was a young woman who wanted to be present, but at the request of the Indians she was asked to remain away.

July 14. Thursday.

The Frenchman who had been wounded Wednesday morning died of his wounds about the same time of night as when he was wounded; he was buried as soon as possible so that nobody outside the Fort might know that he had been killed, but in spite of the precautions which were taken to conceal his death it was known by both the French and the Indians.[94]

[94]This was Jacques Cavelier of Montreal, whose father, also named Jacques, was a master armorer of that place. For Cavelier's arrival at Detroit with a cargo of trade goods see *ante*, 136-37. Although the Indians had threatened to kill both Lacelle and Cavelier if they did not keep away from the fort (Hough, *Diary of the Siege of Detroit*, 23) the latter evidently succeeded in joining the garrison, only to be shot, as our Author relates, in the night of July 13-14. He was buried by the priest in the parish cemetery on July 14, the ceremony being duly recorded in the St. Anne Parish Register.

July 15. Friday.

Nothing of any importance happened.

July 16. Saturday.

A slave belonging to Mr. Beaubien came into the Fort, having been sent by his master to reclaim some live stock which had been frightened by the Indians and had wandered to the Fort.[95] The slave was arrested and imprisoned because, according to rumor, he had been with the Indians firing on the English and upon the sloop.

July 17. Sunday.

Several people who knew perfectly well that this slave was a respectable man and who had known about his conduct at the commencement of this affair came to the Fort to vouch for the pani and secure his discharge, but pardon was refused him till further evidence from other witnesses.[96]

About * * o'clock in the evening Mr. Gamelin came to the Fort with two men, and reported that the Indians planned to attack the French settlers in the surrounding region and asked for arms and ammunition, which were given him. He was cautioned to take good care of himself, and to send the same word to all the settlers; and at

[95]Probably Antoine Cuillerier *dit* Beaubien. The cattle had come to the fort on July 1. See *ante*, 157-58.

[96]A pani (variously spelled) was an Indian slave. The origin of the term is uncertain.

the first gunshot fired in the region men would sally from the Fort to assist them.

Upon receipt of this news the Commandant ordered that all the French who were in the Fort should be under arms the whole night in order to give assistance to the Coasts[97] if necessary. But fortunately the night went by quietly and the settlers got off with a night's vigil and a scare.

July 18. Monday.

The gates of the Fort had been continually closed up to this day for safety and to prevent a surprise from the Indians; this was very bothersome, not only to the officers who were compelled to open them for the needs of those who asked to come in, but also for those who wanted to go out, and through fear of a refusal or of being turned back did not dare ask to have them opened. In order to settle all the difficulties, knowledge of which had reached him, the Commandant ordered that the gate which faced the river should be opened to the public need from nine in the morning to six in the evening; and that two sentinels should be stationed at each side with orders not to allow any French to go out without permission, but to allow all who came to the gate to come in. The Indians were excepted in the order—truth to tell they did not

[97]That is, to the several neighborhoods which in French Detroit were thus designated.

approach nearer than half a mile or so, and then only with many precautions.

During all these days the Indians did not approach to fire upon the Fort.

At one o'clock the Commandant was warned that the Ottawas were engaged in something which deserved attention. They were greatly occupied in building a new fire-float of dry wood which they planned to send down along the river and which, when it was set on fire, should drift upon the sloop and burn it. But it took a long while to get the work ready for what it was designed to do.

Toward nine in the evening some Chippewas came and fired a few volleys upon the sloop, which in turn replied with some balls. After the firing the Indians howled abuse at the guards on the vessel among whom was an Englishman who had formerly been a prisoner of the Ottawas; he spoke the Chippewa tongue pretty well and he replied to the Indians in the same strain.

July 19. Tuesday.

Around two o'clock P. M. Mr. Beaubien brought the news that some twelve savages were hidden in ambush a little more than half a mile away for the purpose of firing upon the Fort. They were discovered in their hiding place and two cannon balls and two shells were discharged at them; one of the latter hit an apple tree into which six Indians had climbed. They came down promptly and fled from the enclosure to their camp, where they kept quiet the rest of the day.

July 20. Wednesday.

The Commandant received news from the Indian camp by which he was again informed that the Indians were at work making something to sweep the river, so as to succeed in burning the sloop that had remained near the Fort and protected the approaches to it; but their work was only in its infancy and it would take a week longer, at least, although they had been at work upon it for four days, and were bound not to come and fire upon the Fort till the fire-raft was done.

At this report the Commandant was minded to profit by the delay in order to save his sloop from the destruction which threatened it. He ordered that two boats be sheathed inside with oak planking five inches thick and that the gunwales be increased to the height of * * feet * * and sheathed like the inside, so that a man standing upright in the boats would be protected from the bullets. In the prow of each boat a swivel gun was mounted so as to rake in three directions; these were tested in the middle of the river in front of the Fort and answered all expectations.

July 21. Thursday.

The Indians, filled with their project, worked as industriously at their fire-raft as if they were paid for it; they did not give themselves any respite, hardly taking time to eat their meals.

From what he had been told concerning the way the Indians went about their enterprises the Commandant judged that he had time enough yet to work upon his barges; he ordered four grappling-hooks to be rigged, two for each boat, one of each pair supplied with an iron chain fifteen feet long, the other hook made of steel or cast iron and attached to ten fathoms of cable. The two boats thus equipped were to go to meet the fire-raft and cast their grappling hooks with the chains upon it, while the other hooks or half anchors were to be dropped; in this way the course of the raft would be arrested and the sloop saved from the danger which had threatened it for some time, and the labor of the Indians rendered useless. During this time the sloop was to weigh anchor again and move nearer the Fort with the help of the cables which were to stop the fire-raft.

Toward evening a rumor spread that the Hurons of the bad band and the Chippewas were plotting to make an attack during the night on the settlers of the Southwest Coast; the settlers stayed on the alert all night, but fortunately the rumor proved to be unfounded.

July 22. Friday.

The day passed quietly for both parties. In the course of the day the news was brought by an Abenaki Indian, who came, according to his story, from Montreal, that a French fleet was coming to Canada to recapture the country; however, the story died in its inception as there was nothing true about it; but even though it was false it reawakened the hope of Pontiac, of his tribe, and of the Chippewas, who had * * * their foolish schemes the fire-raft, the labor upon which * * *

In order to rescue his master who had fallen into the river an employee of Mr. Pierre Réaume wished * * * (Here follow in the Ms, six lines quite illegible.).[98]

July 23. Saturday.

The day passed very tranquilly for both sides. About three o'clock P. M. there was heard in the Fort from the direction of the Huron village a volley of gun shots as if to salute the arrival of some barge. The English feared it was to greet

[98]Schoolcraft, who had the Manuscript in 1846, translated this section as follows: "About . . . a man in the employ of Mr. Beaume [Réaume] wishing to cross the river on his master's business. As he had reached the middle, the Indians made several discharges at him. These made him return with more speed than he had gone. About ten in the evening, as the sentinels were on the watch, random shots were fired."

the coming of some new prisoners, but it turned out to be the arrival of André Huron of Lorette.[99]

July 24. Sunday.

The Indians, who were determined to destroy the sloop, labored hard to carry out their project, and the Commandant, who was equally determined that their project should fail, ordered the two boats I have spoken of before to make a reconnoissance up the river in order to interrupt them in their labors, and it was done. Toward ten o'clock three officers with sixty men well armed embarked in the two boats and a barge and went up the river to discover the place where they were working.

The savages, who saw the three boats in the distance and believed it was some booty coming into their hands, abandoned their labors, and twenty of them with weapons in their hands came out in two canoes to meet the three boats. The English who were aboard allowed them to

[99]Lieutenant Hay's Diary of the siege contains somewhat frequent mention of André (Andrew, Aaron) the Huron as a bearer of messages between Detroit and Fort Pitt and other places, and as a leader of forays against the hostile Shawnees and Delawares of the Upper Ohio area. He was still engaged in such activities in the early summer of 1765. Hough, *Diary of the Siege of Detroit,* index entries. Lorette is the Huron village a few miles outside Quebec which was founded by the band of fugitives who fled from the ravages of the Iroquois in the Georgian Bay area in 1648–50.

come within gunshot. The savages did so, not understanding the construction of these boats; they advanced with cries of joy, thinking they would capture them, but they received a rude surprise. When the commander of the boats saw them near enough for all the shots to carry, he ordered his men to seize their guns and fire not only the muskets but the swivels as well. This startled the Indians, who were not expecting such a salute, and they retraced their course quicker than they had come. From the shore they fired upon the boats and slightly wounded a man in the head with a bullet which pierced his hat and carried away a lock of his hair.

The boats and the barge returned to the Fort about noon without being able to discover either their hiding place or their work. The Indians followed along after them on land as far as Mr. Chauvin's house, a mile and a quarter from the Fort, where the barge discharged a cannon ball at them which scattered them but did not wound any. However, the ball entered the house, doing great damage, and dangerously wounding two savages, one in the arm, the other in the thigh; the latter died some days later.[100]

[100]The Chauvin family has been represented in the Detroit River area from 1726 (possibly earlier) until the present time. Its American founder was a toolsmith who migrated from France to Canada and on Jan. 16, 1696

About one o'clock in the afternoon the Ottawa and Chippewa chiefs repaired to the village of the Hurons in obedience to a request from the chiefs of the Eries and Delawares, who had sent word early in the morning asking for a council.

The Commandant ordered the two boats and the barge around three o'clock in the afternoon to take the same number of men, and go back up the river to where they went in the morning to see if they could discover the Indians and where they were at work. But they were unable to find out anything; the Indians followed them as in the morning and fired upon them. The boats and the barge returned the fire without doing any damage because the Indians took refuge behind the fences. The boats and the barge returned to the Fort about six o'clock no better off than when they left.

Around ten o'clock in the evening the Ottawas came and fired some scattering shots at the Fort.

July 25. Monday.

married at Quebec Mary Cauchon *dit* Duchauteau, a native of that city. Their son Charles, born at Quebec on Nov. 4, 1702, married at Detroit on Oct. 27, 1726 Marie Anne Casse *dit* St. Aubin. He was buried at Detroit on Aug. 17, 1772. Marie Anne Casse *dit* St. Aubin was buried Jan. 17, 1789.

They were the parents of eleven children, one of whom, Charles Chauvin, who was born June 22, 1737, had marital relations with an Ottawa woman. On May 2, 1761 he married Louise Boyer, who was born at Detroit on Jan. 5,

The Ottawas were busy in the council, which was to have been held the day before but had been put over to this day, and neglected the Fort to go to the house of the Delaware and Erie chiefs in the Huron village.

Two residents of the Fort, who had gone on business some time before to the North Coast and had been detained by Pontiac, returned during the day and brought word that the building of the famous raft had been completely abandoned. This was due to the efforts of two Frenchmen who had told them that the boats would hinder the raft from running down the sloop; and that there were grappling chains with two anchors to hold the vessel moored in the middle of the river, and that they were laboring in vain as they would never accomplish their purpose. This discouraged them so that they absolutely gave up their mad enterprise.

The rumor was circulated in the Fort about ten o'clock in the evening that Messrs. Jacques Godfroy and Mini Chêne had returned from the Illinois where they had been sent by Pontiac. The report was not substantiated till the next day.

1745. Both bride and groom lived at the Northeast Coast. Charles, a blacksmith, was buried at River Raisin (modern Monroe, Michigan) Aug. 22, 1821. Either he, or more probably his father, was the individual whose house was bombarded. Data adapted from Dennisen, Detroit Genealogies (Ms.).

July 26. Tuesday. St. Anne's Day.

Early in the morning it was learned that the messengers whom Pontiac, great chief of the nations of the North, had sent to Mr. De Neyon, Commandant of the Illinois country, had returned the night before. Growing out of this all sorts of rumors were circulated by the French in the Fort, but they had no foundation in fact and so died in their birth; the principal one was that the Illinois nations strongly recommended the Indian nations of Detroit not to do any harm to the French who lived on the surrounding Coasts or to those in the Fort, unless they should espouse the cause of the English.[101]

On this day a great council was again held in the Huron village among the Eries, Delawares, Ottawas, and Potawatomies. At its conclusion Pontiac in his capacity of over-chief of all the nations of the North, wearing his war-belt, caught up the tomahawk of battle and began to chant a war-song against the English, at the same time inviting all the chiefs in the council to do

[101]Lieutenant Hay records that Angelique Cuillerier informed her lover, James Sterling, that Godfroy told Pontiac that De Neyon could not send any assistance as yet, since he had heard by a Spanish vessel that the peace was made, but that as soon as his couriers whom he had sent to New Orleans returned, if he found the report to be false he would see what he could do, and that he desired the French settlers to "keep themselves quiet." Hough, *Diary of the Siege of Detroit,* 51–53.

likewise; he told them that the Master of Life had ordered him to make war upon the English and spare not, and the field must be swept clean for the coming of his Father in the autumn. Aroused by his example, all the other chiefs and the Indians chanted the war-song in their turn till the end of the council.

According to the report of some Frenchmen of the vicinity who were present the Erie chief said: "My brothers, remember that the French are our brothers and that they must not be harmed because our Father could reproach us for it unless they should take up the interests of the English."

July 27. Wednesday.

The Indians spent all this day chanting the war-song—each nation in their own village led by their chief; and they took new measures to insure the capture of the Fort, but all their plans amounted to nothing.

Around two o'clock in the afternoon André, [the] Huron of Lorette, whom the English had suspected of being concerned in the uprisings of the Indians and even of being ringleader, came into the Fort to vindicate himself and prove his innocence.

About six o'clock some one came and reported to the English that the savages intended to set fire to the two portable bastions which were situated in the rear of the Fort on the slope and in which four sentinels were posted each day.

July 29. Friday[102].

All night a fog so dense that one could not see a step in front of him. Toward daylight it thinned a little, and about five o'clock, an hour when one was least expecting it, a large number of barges were seen on the river to the right of the River Rouge. The Fort was at once on the alert, thinking it was some Indian parties coming to join the ones here. The English did not suspect it was relief for them although they were expecting some, and to assure themselves as to what it might be a cannon shot was fired on the southeast side. A cannon shot came in response, for these barges had four little cannons mounted as swivels in the bow, and there were in addition two small mortar six-pounders.

When the shot was heard the Commandant, followed by Mr. Hopkins and two other officers, embarked with ten soldiers in one of the boats that I have spoken of before and went out to meet the barges and see what they were. There were twenty-two of them with two hundred

[102]The entry for July 28, now missing from the Manuscript, was supplied as follows in the translation made in 1886: "The Indians did not move this day. [The Commander asked] the settlers to come into the Fort and not go to the shores [to their homes]." See *Mich. Pioneer Colls*, VIII, 337.

eighty troops and six cannons, and an aide-
de-camp of General Amherst was in command.[103]

As the barges passed between the Huron and
Potawatomi villages, which were opposite each
other, they were saluted by volleys from the two
nations which dangerously wounded fifteen men
in the body, two of whom died, and some others
only slightly in the arms and hands. From Niagara to the Fort here the barges had been guided

[103]Captain James Dalyell, the younger son of a baronet,
obtained a lieutenancy in the newly-raised Royal American Regiment in January, 1757. He was subsequently
transferred to the Eightieth Regiment, which General
Gage raised, and in September, 1760 "with the help of
patrons back home" to the First Regiment, an old unit
possessed of social and military prestige. He was also
appointed aide-de-camp to General Amherst. His ambi-
tion to achieve further recognition and promotion led him
to a tragic end. Arriving at Detroit, imbued with General
Amherst's own contempt for the fighting qualities of the
Indians, he prevailed upon Major Gladwin, his superior,
to permit him to lead a surprise attack upon Pontiac's
camp at the Grand Marais. The disaster locally known ever
since as the battle of Bloody Run followed, whose description by our author terminates abruptly midway of the
battle and of his closing sentence, with Dalyell slain and
his body shockingly mutilated. Lieutenant Hay records
that "Young Mr. Campo brought in the body of poor
Capt. Dalyell about three o'clock today (August 1), who
was mangled in such a horrid Manner that it was shocking
to human nature; the Indians wiped [whipped] his heart
about the Faces of the Prisoners." Hough, *Diary of the
Siege of Detroit*, 56–57.

by Mr. Lacelle, a trader of Montreal who had interests in this post.[104]

As there were not barracks enough to lodge all the troops, an order was issued that some should be quartered till further orders on private citizens, according to the accommodations of each one, and this was carried out promptly.

In passing by the way of Sandusky the troops terrified some of the Indians who were living on the outskirts of the village there. At sight of so many men the savages took fright and abandoned their cabins, which were pillaged and burned by the soldiers, and their cornfields devastated.

After the arrival of the troops a rumor was circulated in the Fort that still more forces to the number of four hundred men were coming by the northern route to join the English[105]; but it was not true.

July 30. Saturday.

The Commandant ordered that a part of the canoes which had been lying on the edge of the strand in front of the Fort since the beginning of hostilities should be repaired to be ready for use in case they were wanted.

[104]Jacques Lacelle, for whom see *ante,* 134–35.
[105]That is, by the northern shore of Lake Erie, instead of the route by the southern shore, which Captain Dalyell had followed.

In the evening all the troops assembled on the parade-ground for instruction as was customary, and all the officers, the old as well as the new-comers, were there. It was decided to make a sortie in the course of the coming night with three hundred and some odd men, at the head of whom should be the aide-de-camp who had commanded the troops just arrived, and proceed straight to Pontiac's camp in order to bring him and the savages to account and compel them to make peace. Sabers and ammunition were distributed to the whole troop, which was ordered to be ready at the first call in the coming night.

At two o'clock of this same day the Hurons, who had got wind that some sortie was about to be tried, made a pretense of abandoning their village. At Montreal Point in full sight of the Fort they burned some old canoes and rubbish which was worthless to them, and embarked bag and baggage, even the dogs, and departed down the river as if headed for their winter camp. Several of the French believed this, too, and some one went and told the English, who put credence in the departure without wishing, however, to run the risk of going to the village, fearful of some trick on the part of the Indians. And trick it was, because the Hurons dropped down the river beyond sight of the houses, landed in the woods and concealed their women and children and goods, then came back through the forest to the right of the village and took a position where they could ambush the English in case they came to the village, as had been rumored.

It was a false report, nevertheless the Hurons remained in ambush on the lookout two days, after which they came back to their village just as they had departed.

July 31. Sunday.

About two o'clock in the morning, following the orders of the aide-de-camp, all the troops selected for the expedition were ready to set out in light marching order, stripped to their jackets and carrying their accoutrements and their arms. As soon as they left the Fort they turned in the direction of Pontiac's camp which was at that time about two miles and a half north of the Fort at a place called Cardinal Point[106].

---

[106]Members of the Cardinal family visited Detroit as early as 1708. Jacques Cardinal was born at Montreal July 23, 1685 and married Jane Duguay there Feb. 17, 1715. Their second child, Jacques, was born at Detroit on March 10, 1719, although several subsequent children (down to 1728) were born at Montreal. One daughter, Jane Cardinal, born here on Feb. 28, 1735, married Dominic Jourdain *dit* Labrosse, who is noted *ante*, 103. Jacques Cardinal, our present subject, lived at the Grand Marais on the Northeast Coast, at or in the vicinity of Pontiac's camp. Data adapted from Denissen, Detroit Genealogies (Ms.).

Unfortunately the English had imparted their plans to some French inside the Fort, who had repeated them in confidence to some of the French on the outside, and through these confidences the savages learned of it. They were on their guard; in order not to be surprised they concealed their women and children away from the camp, leaving in it only their old men. Then, as they knew the hour when the troops departed from the fort, they went to meet them in two bands,—one of two hundred fifty going through the woods along the edge of the fields and forming an ambuscade on the farm of Mr. Chauvin, two-thirds of a mile from the Fort; the other band of one hundred sixty men took up a position in ambush at the home of Baptiste Meloche, where their camp had been earlier and where they had thrown up entrenchments which were even bullet proof. Here they awaited the English, who did not think the Indians had been warned of their design.

The troops came on at a rapid march, and in no order, as far as the bridge at Baptiste Meloche's. The Indians could see them at some distance, for the moon was in their favor, lighting up the road the English were taking. Sixty Indians went and occupied Meloche's garden, getting behind the picket fence which faced the bridge. When the savages saw that the head of the detachment had passed a little beyond the middle of the bridge, the sixty poured in a volley which surprised the English who, without changing their marching order . . .[107]

---

[107]Perhaps the best modern accounts of the battle, known ever since as the battle of Bloody Run, are Francis Parkman's *Conspiracy of Pontiac,* I, chap. XV and Howard H. Peckham's *Pontiac and the Indian Uprising,* 201–209. Surprisingly, Lieutenant Hay narrates the battle somewhat briefly. Our Author's account, up to the point where the remainder has been lost, is satisfactory enough, but leaves the recital sadly incomplete. A detailed account of the entire action, written by Major John Duncan of the Forty-fourth Regiment to Sir William Johnson the day after the battle, is in the *Canadian Historical Review,* XII, 184–88 (June, 1931). Duncan had accompanied Dalyell's command to Detroit, but he seems to have remained in the Fort during the sortie.

The ancient river road running eastward from the Fort is today replaced by Jefferson Avenue, one of Detroit's main thoroughfares. Adjoining it are such commercial structures as the home of the Parke Davis Pharmaceutical Company and the plant of the U.S. Rubber Company. Nearby the spot where the ancient highway crossed Bloody Run might be seen, until recent years, the gigantic stove marking the site of the Michigan Stove Company. Shortly beyond (to the eastward) is the entrance to Belle Isle Bridge. Between it and the Michigan Naval Armory lies the tiny river-front park named in memory of Father Gabriel Richard, valiant upholder of morality and education a century and a half ago. To Belle Isle Park, scene of one of the initial atrocities of the Pontiac War, flock scores of thousands of citizens on warm mid-summer days. Within easy sight to the westward the towers of downtown Detroit soar heavenward and farther down river may be seen the mighty span of the Ambassador Bridge,

Here the manuscript ends abruptly. The remainder of the journal is missing.

beside whose either exit once lay the Huron and Potawatomi villages. Both Pontiac's warriors and French habitants have long since vanished from the local scene, although the blood of the latter still flows in the veins of hundreds of Detroit and Windsor citizens.

Now follows an account drawn from standard historical sources of what happened during the remainder of the battle that was in progress when the foregoing Journal ends abruptly; together with a brief sketch of Pontiac's activities to the end of his career.

BLOODY RUN AND AFTER

The Pontiac Journal breaks off, as we have seen, with a final entry dated July 31 describing the early stages of the battle fought at Bloody Run. Since this encounter marks a turning point in the struggle around Detroit, it seems proper to give a somewhat fuller account of its progress and outcome, and to follow with an outline of the later events in the siege of Detroit and the conclusion of the struggle against Pontiac and his allies.

The expedition that became engaged in the Battle of Bloody Run was commanded by Captain James Dalyell, a young British officer eager for action and ambitious to distinguish himself, one who apparently had also a low opinion of the Indian as a strategist in war. Dalyell had arrived at Fort Detroit two days earlier with reinforcements totalling some 260 men. These included Major Robert Rogers and a score or so of provincial troops from New York.

After allowing his men two days of rest, Dalyell secured Major Gladwin's reluctant consent

to move against Pontiac. The force to be used
for the operation consisted of 247 officers and
men, mostly troops he had brought with him.
The men assembled quietly, and left the east
gate of the fort at 2:30 o'clock on the morning of
July 31 to march up the river road. Two gunboats, each mounting a swivel gun, accompanied
the column, to return casualties to the Fort and
cover any retreat that might be necessary.

The sortie was no surprise to Pontiac. Even
before the troops began their march, he had been
warned by his French friends inside and outside
the Fort of what was coming. Against this threat
the Indian leader devised a plan that was to
teach Dalyell something about the red man's
capacity for strategy. Far from planning merely
to repel the attack or win a battle, Pontiac intended nothing less than to cut off the retreat of
the enemy, surround him, and destroy him completely. He sent the main body of his warriors,
numbering about 250, around through the woods
to a point at the Chauvin farm only about two-
thirds of a mile from the Fort. Their task was to
lie concealed until the column had passed, block
the road effectually against any retreat, and
then close in for the work of annihilation.

The smaller portion of his force, about 160
men, Pontiac sent to Parent's Creek, about two
miles from the Fort. Here the savages disposed

themselves about the house and garden fence of a French settler named Meloche, and behind a stretch of rising ground that commanded the bridge that would be used by Dalyell's soldiers.

The Indians held their fire until the forward platoon commanded by Lieutenant Brown reached the middle of the bridge. Then they loosed a blast of fire that wounded Brown in the thigh and laid low a number of his men. Some of their bodies fell into the small stream to redden its waters and give the battle its name. Although the main body of troops behind Brown was also swept by a flanking fire, reinforcements were rushed forward to the bridge and drove the Indians from the ridge. Captain Dalyell himself, meanwhile, had received a slight wound in the thigh.

When Captain James Grant, commanding the rear, heard the firing at the bridge, he knew that battle had been joined. Almost immediately he was attacked from his left, and he sensed the noose that Pontiac was endeavoring to close around the entire expedition. Grant ordered his men to fire wherever an Indian might be, and succeeded in driving the attackers back. He received an order presently from Dalyell to take advantage of all cover on his flank and keep the way of retreat open.

The fighting was by no means confined to the front and rear of the column. The main body

was likewise standing off furious assaults by
Pontiac's warriors. That experienced and wily
Indian fighter, Major Rogers, saw instantly
what was afoot, and quickly ordered a party of
his Rangers into the nearby house of Jacques
Campau which he used as a strong point. By this
means he was able to foil the Indian plan of en-
circlement for at least a portion of the British
column.

Dalyell, no doubt inspired by an entirely new
respect for the Indian military capacity, decided
that the only prudent thing to do was to fall
back toward the Fort. His retreat was held up
for some time at one point by a force of Indians
entrenched behind piles of cordwood and in a
basement excavation. He saw that only a determined frontal assault would clear the way.
Dalyell himself led the attack, and was killed.

As the column continued to fall back along
the road, news came that Major Rogers was now
completely encircled in his "blockhouse." Lieutenant Grant, who had succeeded to the command of the expedition on Dalyell's death,
ordered one of the gunboats to move up and try
to drive off the savages besieging Rogers. Orders
were given at the same time to keep the road
open for Rogers' withdrawal, and by the success
of both measures Rogers and his men were
brought out of their tight spot.

THE PONTIAC TREE

Memento of the Battle of Bloody Run, reproduced from an old-time view. The tree was a huge whitewood which Historian B. J. Lossing in 1860 described as sixteen feet in circumference and still bearing the bullet marks made on it a century before. It was cut down on June 2, 1886.

Thanks to Grant's able management of the retreat, the column, badly mauled, was back in the Fort by eight o'clock in the morning.

The casualties numbered fifty-seven, of whom twenty, including Captain Dalyell, were killed. Three more of the wounded died later. A number were taken prisoners.

The result was unquestionably a victory for Pontiac. He invited some of his French sympathizers to a feast in celebration, and his prestige went up enough to attract some reinforcements from some of the previously lukewarm tribes. Nevertheless, he had failed of his main purpose, which was the complete destruction of Dalyell's expedition.

When it was all over, the Fort remained stronger through the new troops Dalyell had brought, and events were to prove that the chances of the ultimate success for Pontiac's campaign at Detroit were far less favorable than they had been before the battle.

Although the Indians lurked around the Fort in considerable numbers, further troop reinforcements arrived and little happened. Several raids were tried by land and water against the Indians, but without much success. The siege nominally continued; but the long-drawn-out beleaguerment was something the Indians were not accustomed to, and Pontiac's prestige slowly diminished with tribes who might have contributed to his strength.

Although Pontiac had administered a spectacular defeat to the British in the West, the campaign of the Indians in the East had lately been far less successful. On August 5 Colonel Henry Bouquet was attacked by a strong force of Delawares, Shawnees, Mingoes, and Hurons at Edge Hill, a day's march east of Pittsburgh. Confident of eventual victory, the Indians kept under cover and fought a battle of attrition against the troops they now had surrounded completely on the top of a hill. When Bouquet thinned a portion of his line by drawing two companies off within the circle of his defense, the savages thought the end was near, and rushed forward in a wild charge. Bouquet, as a matter of fact, had played a trick on his enemy worthy of the Indians themselves. As the warriors drove in for the kill, the two companies that had been withdrawn suddenly appeared on their flank and poured in a devastating fire. When the Indians tried to fight their way back to the cover of the woods, they were struck hard once again by a strong force of troops. This battle (named after Bushy Run, a mile away, to which the Colonel moved his troops afterward for water) put an end to the worst of the Indian terror in western Pennsylvania.

In 1764 Bouquet led a second expedition into Ohio from Pennsylvania, forcing various Indian tribes to beg for peace and free the prisoners they had taken. It should be remembered, however, that these victories followed upon a long period of plunder and desolation up and down the frontier. Of twelve fortified points attacked all but four were captured, and most of the garrisons were massacred. Pontiac's incitement to destruction and death among the tribes had produced a reign of havoc and death over so vast an area that the record stands among the darkest in the annals of Indian warfare on the North American continent.

At Detroit Major Gladwin continued to skirmish with the Indians in a desultory fashion. The Fort was too well defended to be taken, yet the force at his command was not strong enough to enable him to move against the savages and defeat them decisively.

Sniping and small engagements went on for some time, but without much satisfaction to either Major Gladwin or to Pontiac. The Indian leader suffered more and more defections from the tribes allied with him, and presently a portion of his own Ottawa tribe declared that Pontiac was no longer their leader. The great chief was losing his grip. The French along the river could now sense who was destined to come out on top. It finally became clear even to Pontiac that the help he had so long expected from the French was not to be forthcoming; for at the end of October official word was brought to him that the French nation had signed a peace treaty with the British.

After peace overtures to Major Gladwin in a note signed by Pontiac on October 31, 1763, the siege was ended, and Pontiac withdrew to the Maumee River. There he and the Ottawa families who followed him from Detroit spent the winter.

Pontiac was, however, a man who had the greatest difficulty in reconciling himself to defeat. He continued to plot and conspire with other chiefs for the resumption of the siege at Detroit. He could not get over the idea that help would eventually come from the French, and it is believed that only the lack of ammunition (allowed him by the French only to the extent of his needs for hunting) prevented him from resuming the war in 1764. He spread falsehoods in the effort to keep his influence, and threatened to kill members of the Ottawa tribe who had sought to make peace at Detroit. One of the British officers charged with the pacification of the Indians, Colonel John Bradstreet, held the opinion at one time that Pontiac should be removed from conspiratorial temptation by "maintaining him at His Majesty's expence the remainder of his days." Pontiac was finally induced to conclude a treaty of peace and amity with Sir William Johnson at Oswego, New York, in July, 1766.

Pontiac, one of the most resourceful leaders who ever appeared in the wars with American Indians, was assassinated in Cahokia (nearly opposite St. Louis) by a Peoria Indian in April, 1769. What the reason was for this act is not entirely clear, but it appears to have grown out of the quarrels in which Pontiac was involved with other Indians to the end of his days.

John Rutherfurd's Captivity Narrative

LIEUTENANT JOHN RUTHERFURD

Reproduced from a portrait owned by his great-grandson,
Lieutenant-Colonel R. M. Raynsford of Milton Manor, Northampton, England.

John Rutherfurd's
Captivity Narrative

*Mr. John Rutherfurd's Journal in a letter to
Sir John Nisbet, New York, 1763 Copied at
Wells, October 1st, 1787 by M. Rutherfurd.*

MAJOR GLADWIN of the 80th Regiment,
Commanding Officer of Detroit, being
desirous to know whether the lakes and rivers
between that place and Michilimackinac were
navigable for vessels of a greater burden than
the small bateaux they made use of, by which
discovery Michilimackinac and the little posts
thereupon depending might be more conveniently and expeditiously supplied with provisions
and military stores, ordered Lieutenant Charles
Robertson of the 77th Regiment, who commanded the King's vessels on Lake Erie, to go
with a party consisting of six soldiers and two
sailors in a large bateau with the necessary im-
plements to sound the Lakes. Sir Robert Davers,
who had passed that winter at Detroit (excepting some little excursions he made among the
Indian villages in the neighborhood), having a
curiosity to see farther into the country, which
in fact was the motive that induced him to come

so far as Detroit, accompanied Captain Robertson, and both gentlemen inviting me to go along, I joyfully accepted their invitation as it then had all the appearance of a pleasure jaunt. We promised ourselves excellent sport in shooting water fowl, with which that country abounds, not in the smallest degree dreading any interruption from the savages around us, who but a little before in full council had renewed their profession of friendship for the English and received from them presents to a considerable amount.

We accordingly set out on May 2, 1763, Captain Robertson, myself, and the military party were in the bateau. Sir Robert Davers with a Panee or Indian slave was in a little wooden canoe, being better than a bateau for going into shallow water after game, and so easily navigated that he and his boy were sufficient to cross the lakes and go up the creeks, among the Indian villages.[1]

[1] Sir Robert Davers of Suffolk, England arrived at Detroit prior to April 26, 1762, on which date Captain Donald Campbell reported that he was about to leave Detroit to make a tour of the Lakes. Alexander Henry reported his arrival at Sault Sainte Marie about the end of the same month "on a voyage of curiosity." In September he was back at Detroit, where he passed the ensuing winter of 1762–63. On May 2 he embarked with Captain Robertson upon the exploration of St. Clair River and Lake which terminated in his death in the manner the Author relates. See Alexander Henry's *Travels and Ad-*

ventures (Lakeside Classics ed., Chicago, 1921), 70; letters of Captain Donald Campbell in *Mich. Pioneer Colls.*, XIX, 139, 164.

In Mrs. Anne Grant's oddly mistitled *Memoir of an American Lady*, first published in London in 1806, a strange story concerning Sir Robert Davers is recorded (James Grant Wilson, Ed., New York, 1901 edition, Vol. II, Chap. 14). The author, who was born in 1755, was the daughter of an army officer serving in America. In or about 1758 he sent for his family, who resided in New York and (subsequently) Vermont until 1768. They then returned to Scotland and the 13-year-old daughter never saw America again. Obviously she had no first-hand knowledge of the Pontiac War, but she may well have obtained from her Scottish contacts the information she records concerning Sir Robert. He was (she relates) the sixth son of an ancient English family all of whose older brothers while between the ages of 25 and 30 were attacked by a "hypochondriac disorder," which terminated in suicide. Thus Sir Robert succeeded to the family estate and title, and to the apprehension that in his turn he, too, would fall victim to the fatal malady which had destroyed his brothers. Upon approaching the age when they had perished he resolved to avert the doom which they had met by removing among a people who were strangers to the practice of self-destruction. Migrating to America and finding his melancholy still increasing, he decided to join some Indian tribe, and upon the advice of Sir William Johnson sought out the Hurons living on the Upper Lakes. For two years he lived among them, adopting their native dress and manners. Letters written to friends disclosed he had conquered his hereditary malady and was ready to return to his home, where if his despondency should recur, he would once more rejoin his Huron friends. Unhappily his death at the hands of the hostile Chippewas, as related by our Author, ended any design he may have entertained of resuming a wilderness life.

May 4th, we overtook a canoe with an Indian family in it. We exchanged our bread and tobacco with them for fish newly caught and parted very good friends.

May 5th, we passed several Indian villages, but there appeared to be few Indians at them. We supposed they were out upon their hunting parties but afterwards found that they were on a party of a very different nature, being collected at the place where we were afterwards attacked by them.

May 6th, in the morning we arrived at *La Pinnierre* where there were some Canadians building a sawmill for whom we brought, at the desire of a French gentleman at Detroit, a few barrels of flour.[2] They returned us thanks and told us with all the rhetoric they were masters of

[2]*La Pinnierre*, or the Pinery, on Pine River in St. Clair County was French Detroit's chief source of pine timber for building purposes. About the year 1763 Captain Patrick Sinclair obtained from the Indians a grant of a large tract of land in this vicinity (over 24,000 acres) and on it proceeded to develop a saw mill and other appurtenances of a landed estate. Here for several years beginning in 1780 lived Jean Baptiste Pointe Sable, a mixed-blood Negro, who subsequently removed to the mouth of Chicago River where his long occupancy afforded occasion for the most ancient of Chicago jokes to the effect that the first white man at Chicago was a Negro. See William L. Jenks, *St. Clair County, Michigan*. . . . (Chicago, 1912), I, 92–95; M. M. Quaife, *Chicagou* (Chicago, 1933) 37–38.

that all the nations of Indians around were in league to take up the hatchet against the English; that they knew of our coming that way, and were waiting six miles up the river to seize and destroy us, and if we proceeded any farther we would certainly be cut to pieces. They begged us with tears in their eyes for God's sake to return, and by means of the wind and strong current of the river we might gain the Fort before they could perceive we had discovered their intentions.

This was friendly advice, given by people who showed, even by their countenances, that they had our safety very much at heart, and had we followed their counsel many would have saved their lives on this occasion and others would have avoided a long and dangerous captivity. Captain Robertson partly doubted the truth of what the Canadians told us, and partly through a mistaken opinion that the English upon first acquaintance with Indians are generally too apt to conceive of their bravery, imagined they would not dare to attack us till under cover of the night. As it was then morning he thought that he might go six miles farther and sound about the mouth of the River Huron[3]; which done, his work would be finished, and then return to the

[3]The St. Clair River at present-day Port Huron, Michigan.

Fort as fast as possible. He therefore ordered the rowers to ply their oars, and without seeming to suspect any danger proceeded till we came within six miles of the above river, where there was a small Indian Village, at the same place where the Canadians had informed us we would be attacked by the savages.[4]

Then it was, though alas too late, that Captain Robertson discovered the truth of the information we had got, for the whole bank of the river was covered with Indians to the amount of three or four hundred. Sir Robert Davers, who was at this time considerably before us in his canoe, at the request of the Indians put the head of his canoe on shore and smoked a pipe of friendship (as they called it) with some of their chiefs till we came up. He advised us to row on and pass him, and not to seem to suspect their having a design upon us.

Here I must observe that the river was narrower, and ran so rapid that we were obliged to keep the boat close to the shore, and even there the Indians could walk faster than we could row.[5]

---

[4]The statement "till we came within six miles of the above river" is confusing. The village where Robertson's party was destroyed was near the entrance of the river within the limits of present-day Port Huron.

[5]The rapids, scene of the attack, are close below the entrance of the river. Except for this site it has an average flow of about $2\frac{1}{2}$ miles per hour.

To have attempted to return would have been inevitable destruction to us all; besides, they had all their canoes ready for pursuing us. This we were sensible of, so we kept rowing on, and humored them as much as possible. They crowded about us, men, women and children, giving us the friendly appellation of Brothers, telling us they were glad to see us, and begging us to come ashore and we should have whatever was good, the squaws or Indian women showing us fish, maple sugar, &c, in order to induce us to land. We did not, however, choose to accept of their invitation or presents.

They asked for some of our bread and tobacco, which we gave them. This was only to take up our attention, for all this time they were filing off by degrees, till at last there was not an Indian to be seen. The squaws or Indian women were collected so closely upon the bank of the river, endeavoring to divert our attention by ridiculous stories and immodest gestures, that it was impossible to see what was going on behind them or what the men were about, who were then posting themselves behind a rising ground a little beyond us. When we came opposite that place the squaws, as it had been preconcerted, ran off as fast as they could.

As soon as they were all out of the way the warriors fired upon us at the distance of about sixty yards. Captain Robertson was immediately wounded in the left side, which, showing me, he called to the men to sheer off, but alas! he had just spoken the words when another shot through his body killed him. I then took the helm and endeavored to bring the boat around, but two of the soldiers being now killed, the remaining five could not navigate the boat, and as they neither had their arms ready nor loaded they thought only of screening themselves the best way they could from the enemy's fire; but this was all in vain, for the Indians seeing Captain Robertson killed, and the confusion we were in, rushed upon us and easily boarded us, at the same time, according to their custom upon such occasions, making the most dreadful cries and yellings, what they call the *death hollow.*

They had changed their dress from what it was when they spoke to us as brothers, having at that time their blankets and ornaments on, whereas now they were naked and painted black and red, making a very frightful appearance. Every one of us was seized by our future master, for by their custom whoever first seizes a captive by his hair, to him he belongs, and none may take him from him. I was laid hold of by one whose hideous appearance was enough to have banished any hope of obtaining quarter, but indeed before this I had given up all hope of being saved, and became in a manner resigned to the worst. They immediately scalped Captain Robertson and the two soldiers that were killed, and stripped them naked.

My Master, for as such I was to acknowledge him, at that time dragged me out of the boat by the hair of the head into the water, which took me up to the neck, in danger of my life. However, he brought me safe on shore, and with a rope adorned with trinkets (which they always carry with them to war to bind their prisoners) bound me and delivered me over in charge of his squaw, and then went back to plunder the boat.

All this while, Sir Robert Davers (as I was afterwards informed by his Indian boy, who was with him in the canoe) upon seeing the Indians attack us, endeavored to escape with his light canoe to the opposite side of the river. The Indians called to him repeatedly to come on shore and give himself up to them, and they would not hurt a hair of his head. He paid no regard to them, which exasperated them so much that two of them leveled their pieces at him and brought him down. His body fell out of the boat into the river, which they picked up and brought on shore, cut his head off and buried his body; his head was also buried after the scalp was taken off.

My Master returned with his share of the plunder of the boat, which he laid upon my back; with which, marching through the village, we came to the hut where he lived. We had not been there long when a great many Indians came in and got drunk upon some shrub they had got as part of the plunder, and as I knew that in their cups they often killed one another I thought myself in as much danger as ever. One of them, dressed in Captain Robertson's clothes, came in very drunk and seeing me lying in a corner with my hands tied, gave a *hollow*, calling out *English dog*, and made a stroke at me with his tomahawk which must have killed me had not an Indian more sober, and whom I afterwards found to be the best of them, seized his arm and prevented him, and then turned him out of the hut.

My Master's wife, seeing the danger I was in and knowing the same or more Indians might return to the hut, made me lie down behind her and covered me with skins and furs. Soon afterward the same Indian returned and demanded me from my Master, saying *no English dog should be left alive*, upon which he was turned out a second time and well kicked. Soon after that a party of them came for me, upon which my Master was obliged, in order to save me, to tell them I had been carried to another hut, which satisfied them.

The whole night they kept drinking what little liquor we had brought with us and making a most hideous yelling, dancing, and singing, while they were feasting upon Captain Robertson's body. This shocking piece of barbarity is practiced only by some of the Indian nations to the northward, The Six Nations, who use their prisoners, while alive, much worse than they do, yet never eat human flesh, which *they* do, not for want of food, but as a religious ceremony, or rather from a superstitious idea that it makes them prosperous in war. They teach their children to be fond of it from their infancy.

The next day my Master's son brought some small pieces of the body to the hut and roasted it upon a stick at the fire and endeavored to prevail with me to eat of it, often assuring me that *Englishmen's flesh was very good to eat.* My Master requested me to taste it, telling me I was never to think of going back to the English and so ought to conform to the custom of the Indians. I told him I would obey him in everything he desired me, and even in that if he insisted, but that it was very disagreeable to me, and that that was the only command I would make the least hesitation to obey him in, and begged he would not insist upon it. Thus, by a seeming readiness to obey him I avoided eating the body of my friend; and I believe by showing a desire to please him rather gained upon his affections.

My hands were still kept bound behind my back. This being the second day of my captivity, and not having seen any of the poor soldiers, I concluded they had shared the same unhappy fate as their captain, which added to my uneasiness, fearing that I would not be more favorably dealt with. However, to my great joy and comfort, towards the evening of that day I saw Sir Robert's Indian boy, who told me he knew of some of the soldiers being alive.

This boy, having lived long with the English and speaking the language, made me think he would desire to get free from the Indians, who used him much worse than the English did. I therefore thought I might confide in him, so I laid myself open to him, and told him of a scheme I had formed of our escaping together, which was that we should both get out of our respective huts in the night time, when all were asleep, meet at a certain place agreed upon, and there untie each other, and as he understood traveling in the woods, he would pilot us to Detroit, which was not above eighty English miles from where we then were, and that each of us should bring as much fish as would subsist us upon our journey thither.

He agreed to the proposal and went off with

an intention, as I supposed, of meeting at the place appointed. However, towards the end of the evening I was surprised to see my Master coming into the hut, looking very angry at me, and having a thin wooden post and an axe in his hand. Without saying a word he put one end of the post in the ground and tying the other to the roof of the hut cut a notch in it about two feet from the ground and told me in an angry tone something I did not understand, with signs to me to lie down upon my back; then, taking my leg a little above the ankle, he put it into the notch, against which he tied another piece of stick so close that I could not move myself to turn upon my side, but lay upon my back with my hands tied and the end of the rope drawn underneath my Master's body, who lay with his squaw near me upon a bear-skin. Thus I passed the night like a criminal just before his execution, only with the difference that I had nothing to reproach myself with, having committed no offense against my God or the laws of my country. This treatment gave me good cause to suspect the treachery of the Indian boy, who I afterwards found, had, in order to get his freedom (which he did) disclosed my intentions.

Next morning my Master loosed my leg and by an Indian who spoke English told me he had discovered my intention of escaping and that

and pipe, telling me I should smoke, which I did, and afterwards became fond of it.

The hunting season being at this time past, the Indians lived upon fish, without either bread, butter, or salt. This did not agree with my constitution, so that having suffered much from a dysentery, I became so weak as to be unable to walk for seven or eight days, during which time the old man consoled me by telling me that I should not be eaten if I died of that disorder. Ten days after this my Master returned with his family and after much talk of the success of their arms against the English, how many prisoners they had taken, &c, he looked at me, turning me round about, and seemed surprised to see me dressed *en sauvage*. He asked for my hair, which the old man giving him, he put carefully by. Still my hands were tied, and whenever I had occasion to go out an Indian boy held the end of the rope, and when he brought me in fastened it to the rafters of the hut again.

My Master soon after this untied my hands, often telling me of the impossibility of my escaping. I told him I had no such intention, and feigned a satisfaction with their way of living and a particular fondness for my new dress by which means I secured his good will, as he thought he was sure of me, and that from my being so young I would sooner take to the novelty of their way of life and more easily forget my country and my friends. Certain it is, by this behavior I fared in many respects better than those prisoners who appeared sullen and displeased with their situation, some of them suffering death on that account.

I now frequently saw two of the soldiers that were taken with me, but the Indians did not choose us to have long conferences together. However, these short meetings now and then were very satisfactory. It gives inexpressible pleasure to meet one of our countrymen when in a foreign country; judge how much more so when in captivity with a nation of savages of a different color from ourselves. Happy was I to meet and converse with these poor fellows, who a little before I would not suffer to speak to me without the usual marks of respect from an inferior to a superior. Here there was no distinction; nay, we were glad to find three people of our color. We used often to compare notes with regard to the usage we met from our masters. One of them told me he was obliged to eat of Captain Robertson's body. We would form fifty different ways of making our escape, and immediately reject them all as impracticable.

About the middle of May we were in great distress for want of provisions, owing to the indolence of the savages, who never stir out of their huts to fish or hunt till necessity drives them, which was our case at this time. During four days the wind continued so high that no fish could be taken, as they durst not venture upon the lake with their little bark canoes, which generally are navigated by two men, or a man and a boy, the former standing in the bow or fore part, where there is a pole fixed having a light at the end of it, which attracts the fish, it being in the darkest nights they are most successful. The man in the bow sees the fish approaching and directs the boy how to steer the canoe so that he may strike the fish with a harpoon or three-pronged gig.

In this manner I have seen as much as two men could carry of catfish, perch, and pike taken in two hours' time. Independent of the satisfaction of procuring what is so necessary a part of sustenance among them, it is a great amusement and truly a pleasant sight to see upwards of fifty of these lights moving upon the smooth lake in every direction, while the only sound that is heard is the different cries of wild beasts in the forest. This occasions no apprehension to the fishers, who are out of their reach. I before have observed that the stormy weather had reduced us to our last extremity, viz picking up acorns and boiling them in ashes and water, changing the ashes and water frequently to remove the bitter taste. This was our food till the fifth day, when the wind abating, we got plenty of fish.

The Indians are so accustomed to being reduced to this shift that they think nothing of it, and are always sure to make up their loss. When they have victuals of any sort in their huts they do nothing but eat, smoke their pipe, and sleep. Sometimes they amuse themselves with a game something like our children's diversion of shinty, where the females play against the men and often come off victorious.[6] It is on this occasion that the beaux and belles make their conquests and dress in their best attire. My Master used to dress me out in the richest manner, putting all the ornaments belonging to the family upon me, taking me out to the plain and making me strut about to show myself, when the whole village were assembled, calling out to the people to look at the little white man. At this time I was only made a show of, and not suffered to join in the game.

Towards the end of May we began to make preparations for our voyage to join the rest of the warriors encamped within a few miles of Detroit. For this purpose my Master thought it necessary to build a canoe which he and I did in two days, sufficient to carry all our family for many thousand miles. The evening before our

[6]The game of lacrosse.

departure I was surprised to see my Master seize one of the dogs, of which animals we had several in the hut poking their noses every now and then in our victuals, which they could easily reach as the floor was the only table we had, neither were there stools nor chairs in the hut. This dog (which I was not sorry for) was killed and given over to the squaw, who scraped him as we do a hog in hot water. Then my Master invited all his neighbors, sending a man round the village with a number of little painted sticks, one of which was left with each. Upon entering the hut where the feast is held every one produces his bit of stick and lays it upon a platter provided for the purpose. Each of the guests got a double portion, eating one and carrying the other home in a dish which they bring with them for this purpose. I sat in the corner of the hut a silent spectator of this feast, being looked upon as a slave and unworthy to partake of so fine a repast.

After killing or rather drowning another dog for the purpose of appeasing the evil spirit, as they gave me to understand, we set out next morning in our canoe, making short daily voyages, always landing before sunset and putting up our cabin and cooking our fish, which office fell to my share, as well as cutting wood for the fire. The cabin or hut is soon made. It consists of about twenty young trees set up in the shape of a sugar loaf, and all covered with a kind of matting (which is carried in the canoe) excepting a hole in the top to let out the smoke. Every one carries his or her bed clothes on his back, which is either the skin of a wild beast or a coarse blanket, and all lie down promiscuously, men, women, and children, with their feet to the fire, which is in the center.

The second day of our voyage we came to an island where there was an Indian burying ground. Here we halted, and around a particular grave, which my Master afterwards told me was that of one of his sons, he made us all plant a few grains of corn; which done, we reembarked and went on our journey, which we ended in four days, arriving at a Frenchman's house in the neighborhood of Detroit.

This man, being a friend of my Master, we took up our residence close by his house rather than join the rest of the warriors, who were encamped five miles nearer the Fort.[7] We immediately set about building a large bark house more convenient than those they carry about

---

[7]Pontiac's camp was some distance above the present-day entrance to Belle Isle bridge. Assuming the accuracy of the Author's estimate of distance, Peewash's cabin was somewhere near the lower end of Lake St. Clair. Lieutenant Hay, reporting Rutherfurd's escape from captivity, places it nine miles from the Fort. See Hough, *Diary of the Siege of Detroit,* 56.

with them. Here the fireplace was out of doors,
where I broiled two hours every day, boiling
their kettle with a little fish or Indian corn in it.
This new house we finished in about four days,
the severest part of which work fell to my share,
such as carrying the wood and bark.

Here I must observe that I suffered inexpressible pain from my not having any clothes on,
not so much as a shirt to protect me from the
scorching rays of the sun, which burned my
shoulders and back so much that I was one continued blister, and the palms of my hands were
in the same state from continual working with
the axe. The next piece of fatigue I was put to
was assisting my Mistress in planting a large
field of Indian corn or maize, pumpkins, and
other vegetables. This being finished, my Master
carried me to the grand encampment about five
miles from Detroit. Here I had the pleasure of
seeing Captain Campbell and Lieutenant Mc-
Dougall of the 60th Regiment, who came out of
the Fort at the commencement of the blockade
with Major Gladwin's proposals of peace with
the Indians. To these they would not listen; on
the contrary they detained those two gentlemen
prisoners at a Frenchman's house.

Upon my observing to Captain Campbell that
I thought we might attempt our escape, being
within sight of the Fort, he told me by no means

to think of it, as he was well assured that if any one escaped the Indians were determined to sacrifice those that remained. I frequently made visits to these gentlemen, who belonged to the Ottawa nation. Every day there were prisoners and scalps brought into the camp. The scalp is not, as is commonly believed, the whole skin of the head, but is only the uppermost part of the crown, and must have in it that swirl in the hair which every one has there before it can be approved of as a just trophy of the warrior's achievement.

They at this time brought in Ensign Pauli of the 60th Regiment, who commanded at a small fort on Lake Erie.[8] The Indians came into his fort as friends, and while some of them were smoking a pipe as a token of pretended friendship the rest were butchering his small garrison, of whom they did not leave one alive. This gentleman made a very good Indian, being of a dark complexion, and was much liked by his Master, who soon adopted him into his family, which exempted him from all drudgery.

So great a concourse of Indians being gathered together in the French settlement reduced the inhabitants to great distress for want of pro-

[8]Pauli, who commanded Fort Sandusky on Sandusky Bay, was brought to Detroit by his captors on May 25.

visions. The Indians killed their cattle, sheep, and poultry, and when these failed we were almost starved frequently having nothing for a whole day but a single handful of Indian corn, which we parched in the ashes and ate with a spoonful of bear's grease. I often used to beg for a morsel of bread among the Frenchmen's houses, from whose doors I was frequently turned with an empty stomach. I was not able to bear this as well as the Indians, who, when thus pinched, have a way of girding their bodies with a belt which they continue to straighten as their fast continues to be prolonged.

In this distressed situation my Master prudently resolved to quit the camp, and moved us back to the place where I was taken prisoner. Here we had fish as before, and sometimes a little venison. On our return to this village we halted near the burying ground I have mentioned, and while my Mistress and I were erecting our hut my Master went out and killed a bear, which we ate of most heartily. After finishing our repast I was ordered to put the kettle again on the fire, which surprised me a little as we commonly went to sleep after eating. I ventured to ask the meaning of it, and was given to understand, by looks and gestures, that in the morning I should have the mystery revealed. My Master then cut some of the choicest bits of the bear and put them into the kettle, which was hung over a slow fire, and we went to rest.

At day-break the next morning we were called up, and in a formal, solemn manner walked up to the grave, near which a little fire was made. Having seated ourselves around it, each with our dish in our hand, my Master arose and made a long speech, during which he often pointed to the grave and to me alternately, and at every pause we joined in a sort of chorus by way of approving of what he said. When he had finished his speech he divided the broth and meat among us, and after saying a few words over the grave put a piece of the fat of the bear into the fire and directed us to do the same.

This, I was told, was to appease the spirit of the deceased, who might be offended at my being adopted in his place, for he then told me I was as much their son as if I had sucked these breasts (showing me those of his wife), telling me at the same time to look upon the boys as my brothers, and that my name should be no more Saganash, or Englishman, but Addick, which signified a white elk. Notwithstanding this, I was generally called by my Master's name, which was Peewash. I had three brothers, Mayance, Quido, and Quidabin.

My Master, or rather *my Father* now, frequently took me out hunting with him, which was an amusement I was very fond of. Although this was not the season for killing deer, he was under the necessity of taking a few to subsist his family upon when at the camp with the rest of the warriors. We accordingly set out for the camp when we had cured a few carcasses of venison, which we did by smoking them, having no salt.

In crossing Lake St. Clair it happened to blow pretty hard, so that our little frigate was in danger of going to the bottom with Peewash and all his family. To appease the evil spirit, he cut some handfuls of tobacco small, and threw it into the lake, at the same time making a long speech. Whether owing to the tobacco or not I shall not pretend to determine, but we got safe upon *terra firma,* and as the rain had wet our shirts and blankets we hung them on trees and ran about naked till they were dried. They likewise make use of that plant (tobacco) in thunder storms, throwing a quantity of it into the fire, and while it is burning a squaw drums with a piece of iron on the bottom of a kettle. This, they pretend, prevents any mischief from being done to the family by the lightning.

By this time our corn was grown up about a foot high, so that it became necessary to have it hoed and weeded, which was a severe task upon my Mother and me for six days. I flattered myself that my being adopted into the family would have exempted me from this kind of drudgery, as was the case with most of the other prisoners, but Peewash, having a particular regard for his wife, chose that I should still assist her on many occasions, and she being fond of ease laid the most of it on my shoulders. She frequently made me pound or bruise corn in a large mortar till there was scarcely any skin on my hands, and when I showed them to her she only laughed and told me I should soon be better used to it, and that my hands would become hard like hers, which indeed were neither soft nor fine.

The men think it beneath them to do anything but fish or hunt for the support of their family, and in this they take no more trouble than is absolutely necessary, for they frequently kill the game and leave it till they can send their squaws to carry it home, directing them how to find it by breaking off branches and marking the trees for miles from where the game was killed. Having found it she brings home the choicest pieces and dresses them for her Lord and Master, who generally sleeps till he is called to get up and eat. When he has finished his repast he regales himself with a pipe of tobacco mixed with the leaves of the sumac shrub.

In the meantime the rest of the family are busy roasting fish or broiling steaks, each one for himself. The steaks are broiled or toasted upon the end of a stick as we toast bread and in my opinion this is the most delicious way of eating roast meat. Sometimes our Mother roasted a large piece for the whole family, who never wait till it is thoroughly done, but as the outside becomes a little done, everyone with his knife falls upon it and slices away as it roasts, by which means the pleasure of eating (which is one of their chief gratifications) is prolonged. When soup is made, or rather when they boil their fish or meat, they hang the kettle up out of the reach of the dogs, with the soup in it, for everyone in their turn to drink as they choose. The want of salt made me for some time think whatever I ate was very insipid and tasteless. However, hunger and custom prevailed over prejudice and I soon came to eat as heartily as Peewash himself.

About the 8th of June Lieutenant McDougall with a Dutch trader made their escape into the Fort[9], which caused them to look more strictly after us that were left with them, particularly Captain Campbell, who was shut up in a garret in a Frenchman's house. I frequently visited him with Peewash. One evening he told me he felt unwell, and was prepossessed with a notion that he

[9]Lieutenant McDougall escaped to the Fort in the night of July 1–2. The ensuing interval until the murder of Captain Campbell was but three days.

was to die very soon. I endeavored to persuade him not to encourage a thought so melancholy and dispiriting, but to my great grief and sorrow the first thing I heard next day was that he had been killed.

That morning Captain Hopkins of the Rangers made a sortie from the fort, attacked a party of Indians, and killed one of the chiefs of the nation to which I belonged. The friends of the deceased were resolved to be revenged by killing an English captive. This they could not do more conveniently than by murdering poor Campbell, who belonged to the Ottawa nation. That Nation, in their turn, was enraged against the Chippewas for killing their prisoner, whom they were fond of, and resolved upon having satisfaction, which could only be obtained by sacrificing a prisoner belonging to the Chippewas of rank equal to that of Captain Campbell, the better to compensate the loss. Accordingly they pitched upon Ensign Pauli, but he being informed of his danger by a handsome squaw who was in love with him, assisted by her escaped out of the Frenchman's house; from whence with much difficulty he got into the fort after being fired at several times by the sentries, who took him for an Indian.

The Ottawas, being disappointed in their design upon Pauli determined to take my life, being, as they thought, next in rank to an officer, and superior to any of the private soldiers they had among them. Peewash, hearing that they were in search of me, took me to a Frenchman's barn and covered me with straw, in which situation I lay for the space of three hours, expecting every moment to have the tomahawk in my skull; till a party of Indians, with Peewash at their head, came and took me out of the barn. Notwithstanding his assuring me I was not to suffer death, I could not help being alarmed and doubtful of my safety.

They marched me as a prisoner for four miles till we reached the grand encampment, which was in the middle of the French settlement. Here in the road was lying a dead body, mangled and scalped, which the dogs were eating. They made me stop for a considerable time, and looked at it with much seeming satisfaction, at the same time, in an exulting tone of voice, telling me that there lay our Chief, our *Great Chief,* Captain Campbell. Indeed, it would not have been possible for me to have recognized that it was the remains of my good friend. He was scalped and his ears, nose, an arm, a leg and other parts of his body cut off. It was a very shocking spectacle to me, yet however disagreeable, I was obliged to view it.

They then led me into a great hall in a Frenchman's house, in the court yard of which there were about two hundred Indians of different nations. In the middle of the hall a small table and five chairs were placed, in four of which sat the chiefs of the nations encamped around Detroit; the fifth chair was for myself, who at that time would gladly have dispensed with this mark of distinction.

They then produced some letters written in English, and Pontiac, the leading man of the four nations, told me by a French interpreter that as I could speak French and read English writing they had pitched upon me to explain what was in these letters; which he ordered me to do, without concealing any part of them, threatening me with death if I did not read them verbatim as they were written.

Then one of the prisoners, a native of Virginia, who had been fond of an indolent life and married among them, told me that he could read English and would overlook the papers and discover if I attempted to conceal any part of them, adding that the consequence would be my being scalped on the spot.

I accordingly set to work and read the letters in French to a Frenchman, who explained them to the Indians. They were only some old letters that Captain Campbell had in his pocket when he was killed, and a few letters to him from his friends at Detroit while he was a prisoner, sent from thence by a Frenchman who, instead of delivering them, had kept them.[10]

There were several French gentlemen in the hall, who were all as eager about reading the letters as the Indians. What both French and Indians wanted to know was whether peace was declared with France or not. It had been publicly declared by Major Gladwin in Detroit long before that time but the Canadians could not bring themselves to believe that *Le Grand Monarch* would ever cede their country to Great Britain and they still flattered themselves that if they could excite the savages to maintain the war against us for a little while, a reinforcement might come to their assistance from France and that the English might be driven out of Canada, and they were in hopes that there might be something in the letters that might favor their design.

Accordingly they always told the Indians that Major Gladwin had only declared peace in order to prevent their making war upon the English. The letters, however, contained nothing that I thought could favor their design; notwithstanding, they found means to construe them differently, and at least made the Indians more doubt-

[10]Since Captain Campbell was killed on July 4, this meeting must have been held but a day or two later. No report of it has been found in other accounts of the siege. The site of the conference was probably the house of Antoine Cuillerier *dit* Beaubien.

ful of the truth of what had been told them by Major Gladwin. When I had done they all thanked me and appeared satisfied with my proceedings and gave me leave to return home with Peewash, who told me he was glad he brought me off so well.

The next memorable circumstance that happened to me was my being sold to Monsieur Cuillerier with whom I had been well acquainted before my captivity, and during it had been frequently at his house (which was only two miles from Detroit) with Peewash in order to get a little bread and salt. In these visits I proposed to Monsieur Cuillerier to endeavor to purchase me from Peewash, who I knew was covetous and fond of riches in the Indian way of estimating wealth, which consists of possessing a profusion of trinkets, such as wampum, beads, bracelets, and silver gorgets.

This gentleman, on account of Mr. Sterling with whom he was very intimate, and who afterwards married his daughter,[11] was much my friend. He made several offers to Peewash for me, by bringing with him a horse and a cow, thinking they would do, as he had often said that he

[11]Sterling married Angelique Cuillerier on Feb. 18, 1765. Since Rutherfurd's Journal was written soon after his return to New York in the autumn of 1763, this statement is obviously an interpolation of the copyist.

liked the white people's manner of living and enjoying such comforts; but he had a greater liking for me than to part with me at so small a price. However, he agreed to let me go for certain merchandise, such as he should choose, to the value of £40, upon condition that I was always to live with Monsieur Cuillerier and not to be allowed to go back to the English.

This we both promised, although we only intended to keep it so long as it would be attended with no risk to my benefactor to break it, for rather than that he should suffer I was resolved to live with him, although at the risk of being again seized by the savages. My mother and brothers took a very affectionate leave of me and went home loaded with the goods they had got for me, leaving me overjoyed with my change of situation. I immediately threw away my dirty, greasy, painted shirt, which I had worn for two months without ever being washed. I scrubbed myself for two hours with soap and warm water to get the grease and paint off. Then dressing myself *en Canadian* with a clean French shirt and long ruffles, a new breech clout, with a mantlet exactly like our lady's bedgown, and a pair of new leggings I began to feel somewhat comfortable.

This Frenchman, being a brother to the former French Commandant[12] and a very great favorite of

[12]More correctly, the two men were half-brothers.

the Indians, they had favored him a little by not killing all his stock, such as cattle, poultry, &c. So I got a good supper genteelly served up, went to a good bed which was provided for me, and slept better than I had done for a long while before. I awoke next morning happy in the thought of being out of the hands of the savages and once more, as I imagined, restored to liberty, thinking there was no doubt I would soon be among my friends in the Fort or, at the worst, to live with such a good family till the war ended would be but a slight hardship. But how fleeting are the joys of this life, and how uncertain are we weak mortals of what it may please the Almighty that we shall suffer in this state of trial and probation. I was happy at this moment beyond expression, and in the next I was doomed to misery.

Before sunset, as I was enjoying the company of the amiable Mademoiselle Cuillerier lamenting together the miserable situation of many poor captives that were still in the hands of the Indians and contriving methods for the deliverance of some of them, a party of armed Indians entered the house, all of them Ottawas and consequently strangers to me, and without saying a word to me or any of the family seized me in a rude manner and brought me down stairs. Then, indeed, my situation wore a very gloomy appearance. I was hurried away from that good family without having time to say more than farewell to them, who, on their part, were as much amazed as myself.

They dared not interpose in my behalf, nor attempt to save me. The ladies of the family burst into tears, crossed themselves several times, and, I believe, fervently prayed for me. All that Monsieur Cuillerier could say to me was to desire me to keep up my heart, and trust *en le Bon Dieu.* As we passed by the French houses all the inhabitants were pitying me, saying what a sad thing it was to behold so young a lad come to so untimely an end; others were calling to me to keep up my spirits, saying there were still hopes, &c,&c. As for myself, I own I was at first much shocked when they seized me, but by degrees I became more resigned, and began to think seriously that my time was at last come, and the dangerous escapes I had made were as so many warnings to me to prepare for that change which we must all undergo, sometime or other.

They carried me to Pontiac's hut, the chief of the Ottawas, who, after leaving me in suspense for some hours, procured a French interpreter who informed me the reason he took me from Monsieur Cuillerier was because several Dutch traders had got Frenchmen to buy them, or rather ransom them as I had done, and if he suffered that trade to go on they would soon have no captives; therefore he was resolved either to keep us all, or else our scalps, for which reason he had ordered all that had been so bought to be taken from them that had purchased them, and that he had resolved to keep me for himself.

This speech eased me in some measure of the disagreeable apprehensions I was under, and gave me reason to hope that my last hour was not so near as a little before I had imagined, yet I wished again to be in Peewash's family. However, this night I remained with Pontiac, but early the next morning the Chippewas, the nation I formerly belonged to, sent a party to take me from the Ottawas; but Pontiac having somehow taken a liking to me (I believe owing to my youth, for they seldom grow fond of elderly people who have the misfortune to fall into their hands, from a belief that they never will be reconciled to their manner of life) refused to deliver me up, the consequence of which refusal had nearly been a war between the two nations.

This was prevented by Wasson, the chief of the Chippewas. After a good deal of altercation upon the subject, Pontiac thought it most prudent to deliver me up, and thereby avoid a war with a nation superior in numbers to his own, which besides the possibility of destroying his own nation would have infallibly ruined the common cause for which they were united. I was immediately carried off by King Wasson to his hut. He was very good to me. He gave me plenty of victuals, and he told me he had plenty of girls in his family to do all the work, so that I should never be asked to do anything, but live as he and his sons did.

This pleased me very much, and indeed the behavior of him and his family was such that I had reason to think myself fortunate in falling into his hands. Every member of the family, which was very large, vied with one another to show me the most countenance and favor, and when any disturbance or alarm appeared in the camp, such as the young fellows, out of mere wantonness or in a drunken frolic, killing any of the captives, which they too frequently did, I was always hid till the danger was over.

The old King became so fond of me that he offered to make me his son-in-law when I should be disposed for matrimony and should fancy any of his daughters who were reckoned the handsomest in the camp and had more wampum than any others. He was satisfied with my telling him that I thought myself highly honored by the proposed alliance, and although I was not inclined to take a wife at that time I did not know how soon I might wish to change my condition, and that then I should be happy to choose one of his family. Little did I suspect that the ease and tranquillity I then enjoyed would be of so short duration. I had not been in this situation for ten days when Peewash expressed a desire to have his son back again with him, saying that he and his wife had heartily repented their selling me to the French gentleman, and they were willing to return the merchandise they had received for me providing I was again restored to them, adding that it grieved their hearts to see me in the possession of another.

Wasson, however great his desire to keep me in his family, knew that although he was the chief of the nation he had no power to keep what was another's property. He likewise did not choose to expose himself or his family to the revenge of Peewash, who would take the first opportunity to resent the injury done him. He therefore was obliged to give me up to my Father, who with his whole house received me again with joy and the most expressive marks of satisfaction; while that of Wasson seemed sorry to part with me, and even the princesses showed that they were not indifferent.

The number of prisoners increased every day. Towards the end of July they had upwards of fifty, besides a great number of scalps that were daily brought into the camp; they were every day murdering some of their prisoners, even

those that had been as long among them as myself. One day, in particular, I was in the hall of
a Frenchman's house which was crowded with
Indians when some of the young warriors brought
eight naked captives into the hall, at the sight of
which I was surprised and terrified. I asked an
Indian who was of the same nation with myself,
and who had frequently professed a regard for
me, whether or not I was to fall a sacrifice with
those they were about to murder. At this question he was amazed to see me there, and without
making any answer he hurried me through the
crowd, and putting me into another room in the
house charged me to lie close and make no noise,
otherwise I would be discovered and killed. He
then locked the door and left me to think on what
had passed.

I found two Dutch merchants in the room in
the same situation as myself, having been hid
there by their masters, who were desirous of
saving them from the fury of their brethren. During our confinement we heard the Indians making
long speeches over the unhappy people that
were to suffer, telling them it was in order to
make them prosperous in the war against the
English that they were to be killed. The poor
victims were begging the French people, who
were looking on, to intercede in their behalf.
One little boy in particular, a drummer of the

Rangers about twelve years old, was crying bitterly and imploring their mercy, but alas he knew not how vain it was to ask it from wretches whose hearts were steeled against every feeling of humanity.

I ventured to crawl to the window, where I saw them lead to the riverside (which ran just by the house) eight of these poor creatures one by one whom they put to death on the spot. Some of them were tomahawked, others they shot with their guns, and some of them they made the little boys shoot with bows and arrows in order to accustom them to cruelty and perfect them in the use of that weapon. Thus they prolonged the pain of these unhappy wretches and when one fell the multitude would set up the most dreadful yells and cries that can be conceived. When they were all dead they scalped them and some of the Indians took the skin off their arms to make tobacco pouches of, as they had formerly done with Captain Robertson and Captain Campbell, leaving the first joints of the fingers by way of tassels.

Then they threw the bodies into the river that they might float down to the Fort, where their countrymen might see what they said they should all undergo in a short time. When this tragic scene was at an end the Indian that had hid me came and set me at liberty, first leading me publicly through the middle of the crowd to convince me that there was no more danger at that time. Then he delivered me to Peewash, who seemed very happy to see me safe, having heard that the warriors had been upon the hunt for me to destroy me.

The following reason was given for this last instance of their barbarity. An old squaw, the wife of a chief, dreamed that she saw ten Englishmen killed and scalped. This she told to the young warriors, who wished for nothing more than a pretext to make a frolic of that sort. She conjured them at the same time to make her dream come true, otherwise, she assured them, they would never prosper in war. This, with a great deal more enthusiastic stuff mixed in her speech, excited their passions to such a degree that they flew immediately about the camp like mad men to collect ten of the prisoners in order to kill them in the manner I have related, to verify the dream of that imp of hell.

However, they were partly disappointed in their design, as all those who had any regard for their captives concealed them. The little drummer was the favorite of an old squaw who wanted much to save him, but notwithstanding her tears and earnest entreaties the young fellows tore him from her arms, declaring that upon such an occasion they would spare neither age nor sex.

Almost every day exhibited fresh instances of their barbarity upon some of the prisoners, so that I lived in continual terror, expecting that every day would be the last. I therefore resolved to attempt escaping at all risks.

There lived a Frenchman near where we had our cabin named Boileau. This man had been civil to me upon several occasions, and I thought he might be of some assistance to me in making my escape. I therefore sounded him upon the subject and found that a little money would go a great way with him. Accordingly I promised to reward him if he would assist me, and thereby gained him to my service. As the French were admitted into the fort, I gave him a letter to my friend, Mr. Sterling, who likewise promised him a reward if he should succeed in delivering me from my captivity. Major Gladwin and several other officers also assured him of their countenance.

When he returned with a line from Mr. Sterling I found him ready to engage in my interest. I therefore redoubled my entreaties and promises in case of success. A scheme for my departure in the most secret manner was next to be fixed upon. We formed many but rejected them all upon more coolly considering the matter. Our eagerness, he to enjoy the promised reward and I, what was more important, my liberty, made it difficult for us to determine upon the most practicable way of effecting it.

However, we at last determined upon the following plan: In the evening we should fix upon he was to embark in his canoe, giving out publicly that he was going fishing as usual; instead of which, he was to go about two miles down the river nearer the Fort and at a certain point of low land which was covered with rushes he was to push into the place in the dusk of the evening, when the Indians would not perceive him, and so conceal himself. I, on my part, was to make the best of my way to him in the night, where he would lie waiting for me.

This plan we were to put into execution the following night. However, on this and several preceding nights the Indians were alarmed by a report that the Chippewas were to be attacked by our forces, which actually happened a few days afterward. Captain Dalyell, who had just brought a reinforcement to the garrison of Detroit, in the night of July 30-31 made a sortie with a strong body of men with the intention of surprising the hostile camp. But the Indians, who had been warned of his design by the French, lay in ambush and attacked him with great spirit; nay, upon this occasion they did what savages were never known to do, they threw themselves into the houses and annoyed the British troops very much from there and from behind fences. The battle continued doubtful for some time but at last our troops were obliged to retreat, which they did in good order to the Fort, leaving upon the field Captain Dalyell and about sixty private soldiers.[13]

Peewash knew nothing of the intended attack till the firing of the artillery and small arms roused him from his sleep. As soon as he heard it, he got up in a great hurry and put on his powder horn and pouch. He then tied my hands, lest in the confusion I should make an attempt to kill the women in the family and make my escape, after which he took his gun and ran as hard as he could to join the army with his party, which was about two miles from where we lived. About two hours afterward he returned to us, overjoyed with the success of the day, giving a most pompous description of the battle and making out that vast numbers of British soldiers were killed, while only six of the Indians had fallen. He likewise told me that our *Sugema*, or great chief, was slain, meaning Captain Dalyell.

I was now unbound and sent to another hut for a large wooden mortar to pound corn in. The

[13]Two officers and 18 private soldiers were killed; 3 officers and 34 privates were wounded. In addition, several soldiers were captured. The Indian loss, although unknown, was probably small.

Indian to whom I went for it had likewise been in the engagement, and was boasting of his feats prodigiously. He told me he had taken the heart of our great warrior, which he would soon feast upon, showing me poor Dalyell's heart roasting at the fire, pieces of the fat of which the young men took off and in my presence rubbed it on the mouth of a poor soldier of the 60th Regiment whom they had taken prisoner. This and other barbarities committed upon prisoners taken in the action shocked me so much that I went directly to Monsieur Boileau's under pretence of bringing some bread to our hut, and agreed to meet him the next night at the place appointed, after having repeated and enlarged my promises of reward to him.

When the evening came I lay down as usual upon my bear skin to sleep, putting off all my ornaments, wampum, silver bracelets, collar, etc. About the middle of the night when I guessed that the family were all fast asleep I crawled out of the hut on all fours. When I was outside I stood at the door for five minutes to hear if they were stirring, but as everything was still I thought this was my time to set off, which I did as fast as my feet could carry me, directly to the woods. I had no other clothes than my shirt, not even daring to put on a pair of moccasins to save my feet, for if the family had happened to awake they would immediately have come to the door after me, and if they had found me dressed they would not be long in discovering my intention.

In all my life I never saw such a night of rain, thunder, and lightning. It was so dark, and the woods were so thick and full of briars and thorns that I was very much retarded in my progress. I could scarcely make more than a mile in an hour. I therefore resolved upon a new method and quitting the woods I went to the river which was hard by, in which I thought I could walk with the water up to my chin, so that the Indians on the road could not see me. This plan would have succeeded had I had more time, but I had yet four miles to go before I could reach the Frenchman and was in danger of being surprised by daylight.

I therefore resolved to take to the woods again, but I was within an ace of being prevented, for just as I was going ashore I saw two Indians with their guns in close conference. They passed by on the road within twenty yards of me. Fortunately there was an old tree which had fallen into the river close by me, behind which I immediately squatted, but I could not conceal myself altogether, so that they must have seen me had they looked that way. If they had observed me I never would have gotten out of that spot alive. I knew this and was in dreadful apprehension, as several soldiers attempting to escape were caught, scalped, and tomahawked on the spot. But these Indians, fortunately for me, were engaged in earnest discourse and were returning from a feast a little intoxicated. I saw them go into a little French house about one hundred yards from me. I immediately ran to the thicket, making as little noise as possible, and to prevent the whiteness of my skin from discovering me to the Indians I rubbed myself all over with black moss and mire.

Thus pursuing my journey in fear and hope, starting at every rustling among the leaves and often mistaking trees for Indians, I at last arrived at the place where I thought the Frenchman would be waiting with the canoe, but could not find him. I ventured to call out in a low voice, but nobody answered. I then began to exclaim against the perfidy of the Frenchman, who in my desperate situation, I thought, had deceived me. Being much exhausted with fatigue, I sat down to rest, hardly knowing what I did. My thoughts were occupied about the Frenchman who, upon reflection, I thought would not be such a coward as to abandon me when he knew that I had to go through the most dangerous part of the enterprise myself. I considered, likewise, that it was to his interest to carry out our agreement. Recollecting myself a little and looking around me I discovered what my anxiety and eagerness had made me overlook, that I was about a quarter of a mile higher up the river than the place we had appointed.

This discovery gave me fresh vigor and spirit. I soon reached the right place, and to my inexpressible joy I found the man asleep in his canoe. After waking him we embarked and pushed to the middle of the river in order that the current might carry us down. We passed through the middle of the enemy's camp, making as little noise with our paddles as possible. We could plainly hear them talk, and saw some of them dancing and singing at a feast around a fire. About an hour before day-break we arrived on board a ship lying opposite to Detroit.[14]

Then it was that I was agitated in a manner I had never before experienced. It would be in vain to attempt to give an idea of my feelings on this occasion. In the morning I went to the Fort where my friends were overjoyed to see me, although I cut a very odd figure among civilized people. The whole town, inhabitants as well as the garrison, turned out to see me. My appearance was sufficient to excite their pity as well as

[14]In a letter written to his Uncle from Niagara on August 20 (copied in the Henry Rutherfurd large notebook) Rutherfurd stated that he escaped from the Indians on August 4. Apparently he arrived at the Fort on the morning of August 5.

their laughter. I had on nothing but an old greasy, painted shirt, my face was painted red, black, and green, my hair had been cut off, and my body was black with the moss I had put on. My thighs and legs were so torn by the briars and thorns and so affected by the poisoned vines that they were swollen as big as any grenadier's in His Majesty's service.

Monsieur Boileau went home as soon as he had put me on board the ship, fearing that if he did otherwise he would be suspected of having aided me in my escape, and this was the last sight I had of him. Mr. Sterling by my order gave him goods to the value of £23- which, with the £39-10- given by Monsieur Cuillerier when he bought me (of which scarcely any was returned when I was retaken) amounted to £62-10 Pennsylvania Currency, which is equal to £39 Sterling.

After I had been about ten days in the Fort and had got the better of my fatigues (though not of the paint) one of the vessels sailed for Niagara to obtain a supply of provisions for the garrison. Mr. Sterling had obtained leave of Major Gladwin to have a considerable quantity of goods that were lying at Niagara brought to Detroit in the vessel, and having no proper person whom he could trust to oversee their safety he applied to me. I knew that bringing up these goods would be of considerable advantage to the Company and wishing to do what little was in my power for the advantage of a company with which my Uncle was connected I agreed to run the hazard, and accordingly embarked on board the sloop.

We had some shots fired at us by the Huron Indians going down the river, which we returned. In four days we arrived at Fort Schlosser near the Falls, and marched under a strong guard to Niagara without any interruption from the enemy. It was late before the sloop was loaded and ready to sail again. Some artillery stores and provisions with about 18 officers and soldiers of the 17th and 46th Regiments was the chief loading.

We had only sailed one day when the vessel sprung a leak and was half full of water before it was discovered. All of the pumps were of little use, so that after throwing all the heavy artillery and some other things overboard we found the only way to save our lives was to crowd sail for the land and run the vessel on shore, but every one seemed to think she would go to the bottom before we could reach land.

Dread and consternation was painted on every countenance and I was surprised to find myself the least moved of all, which must have been owing to my having been for some time so much exposed and inured to danger. While some were stripping themselves to swim, others cursing and swearing at their companions for not working, others praying, and some drinking brandy, I looked tamely on, after finding I could be of no assistance.

When we were at the worst and everyone thought we were going down, our boat, which was our last resource, broke adrift. Our prospect was now truly dismal, expecting every minute to sink or be dashed to pieces on the rocks. I may truly say that the cries and shrieks of a naval officer's lady with three children affected me much more than my own condition. It was a pitiful sight indeed. The mother held two of her children in her arms while the other little innocent was making a fruitless attempt with her hands to stop the water from rushing in the cabin, already some three inches deep. She did this, she said, to prevent the water from drowning her mama.

At last, to the inexpressible joy of all on board, the vessel struck upon a bank of sand within fifty yards of the shore. The difficulty now was how to get ashore, where we had much reason to wish ourselves, as we feared the high surf of the lake would dash us to pieces. In this situation we would have been much at a loss had not Captain Montresor of the Engineers bravely undertaken to swim ashore. Although the distance was great with a high sea and the danger of

Indians being there, he accomplished it and brought the boat back, by which means we all got safe to land.[15]

Expecting the Indians would attack us, we fortified ourselves the best way we could with the barrels of provision. The necessity for this soon appeared, for we were soon attacked by a large body of them who had watched our motions for some time, waiting till we should be more off our guard, which we in fact were at that time.

Several of us were walking along the shore of the lake when we were alarmed by the cries of the savages, which made us take to our heels and endeavor to gain the breastwork as fast as possible. I very nearly fell into the hands of the

[15]John Montresor, born in 1736, was bred to military life from his boyhood. He came to America in 1754 to serve under General Braddock, and for practically a quarter of a century thereafter performed arduous and at times distinguished service in the engineer branch of the army. The exploit related by Rutherfurd, unnoted elsewhere, was quite in keeping with his character and lifetime service. For sketch of his career see *Dict. of Am. Biog.* For bibliography of his activities and writings see "Captain John Montresor in Canada," in *Canadian Hist. Review*, V, 336–40.

The site of the wreck of the *Michigan* has been identified as at Catfish (Eighteen-Mile) Creek on the south shore of Lake Erie. For a more adequate account of the affair, by Lieutenant Montresor, see Royal Soc. of Canada *Transactions*, Ser. I, Vol. XXII, Sect. II, 8ff.

enemy again upon this occasion, as I had happened to stray from the rest of my companions. They rushed out of the woods upon one poor soldier of the 60th Regiment who happened to be nearer them. He knocked down the first savage who reached him but the second cut him with his tomahawk, which felled him to the ground. Neither that nor their scalping deprived him immediately of life. As soon as the Indians left him for dead, he got up and staggered toward the foot of the hill. The Indians were still firing upon us and not a man dared venture to bring the poor fellow up the hill, who by this time had become insensible. We frequently called him but he paid no attention and wandered a little farther, where some days later when the Indians were gone we found him dead under an old tree.

For my own part I had much ado to regain the top of the hill. I was hotly pursued, and in my flight in scrambling through the bushes both my shoes fell into their hands. This was a loss I regretted but little. As soon as we reached the breast-work they fired very hot upon us, which we returned. Our works being very open, we had several of our men killed. The Indians left us the next day but we were detained upon this spot, which we called Lovers Leap, for twenty-four days before we could get a reinforcement of bateaux to carry us back to Niagara. It was here I first entered upon duty as a military man. Every one took his turn of duty as a common soldier. We marched over the carrying place at the Falls of Niagara just three days after the Indians had defeated our troops, and saw there about eighty dead bodies, unburied, scalped, and sadly mangled.[16]

When at Niagara I resolved to tempt fortune no longer in the woods, and determined to go to New York. I arrived here a few days ago, where I expect to remain for some little time with my Uncle and afterwards join the 42nd Regiment, in which I have just got an Ensigncy, preparing for an expedition against the Shawnee and Delaware Indians to the westward under the command of Colonel Bouquet.

I feel not a little pleased to join the army at this time, as I shall have an opportunity, perhaps, of seeing the savages get a complete drubbing and be instrumental in restoring peace and tranquillity to the poor people in the back settlements of this country, where we hear they are committing great ravages and cruelties upon the inhabitants, sparing neither sex nor age.

[16]These were the victims of the Devil's Hole Massacre of Sept. 14, 1763. Since the *Michigan* was wrecked on Aug. 28, the stay of the survivors at the site must have been somewhat less than twenty-four days.

I wish you may be able to understand this long, ill-written narrative, which I have written in a great hurry, as when I began I had no idea that I should have swelled it out to the size of a pamphlet. However, if I had had more time, I don't think that I should have put it into much better language, for having so long been confounded with hearing and speaking different languages, French, Dutch, Chippewa, Ottawa, &c &c that it is no wonder I should be at a loss to write or speak that of my native country.[17]

I am yours &c

[17]Rutherfurd served in the 42nd Regiment (the Black Watch) until the close of the American Revolution. The British army lists record that he became a lieutenant in the Regiment on March 31, 1770 and a captain on August 18, 1778. Following his retirement he resided upon a small property, Mossburnford, in Roxburghshire, Scotland until his death in his eighty-fourth year, January 12, 1830. He was twice married and left descendants by both unions.

Index

INDEX

The Lakeside Classics